FROM LOW *to* GLOW

From Low to Glow

Shaping the Rhythm of Creation by Self-gift

Adeline Nukuna, MD, PhD

First Published in the United States of America in 2020 by Adeline Nukuna

ISBN: 9780578784588 (Paperback)

Cover Photo: Brady Knoll
Cover designed by Spears Media
Designed and typeset by Spears Media Press LLC

To my mother,
Mrs. Florence Nukuna nee Gwanmesia,
who in me instilled deep values,
taught me appreciation day-by-day,
and resilience when times turn tough

CONTENTS

PREFACE

Trials and tribulations are inevitable and adversity may leech on like a parasite, take central place in the mind and the body, displacing everything else. This takes you down so low that you can lose the ability to peep to the light of rebounding resilience in order to rise above the gloom. This book is written to help you up, to project light in your darkest hour, aid you up to serenity, and to mastery over the suppressing realities. It would have served its purpose, therefore, if it uplifts, empowers and opens up avenues for you to discover the alternatives to doom and thereby effect a sense of fulfillment and from low to glow, live and enhance the harmony of the rhythm of creation.

Since words are no more than words until matched by action pitched in authenticity, this work is made genuine by experiential details. Thrust with simply narrated personal life involvements, thrust especially with pain from which a rebound entails coming to terms with those low moments and ensuing glow. The resultant lessons are this way seen as joining in the rhythm of creation concluded by harmony with the self and others through selfless service. The admonished need for achievable goal setting this way syncs with the universal goal of mankind borrowed of the divine, and self-gift is convincingly the finale of all goals.

CHAPTER ONE

OPPORTUNITIES DISGUISED

If one bluntly asked: Are challenges bad moments? Are difficult Moments Bad? Such questions would spontaneously set anyone wondering why they should be asked in the first place. The questions are but rhetorical, their answers all too obvious. Condescending at the risk of being boring to answer, the quick response would be: "Of course, challenges and difficult moments are not welcome any day; they are anathema, detestable, unwelcome and obviously bad". A response like that is dead right, for bad moments are bad moments; finished!

Challenging moments are tough, difficult moments, acrid in all the taste they exude of harsh reality. They are certainly not nice, these challenging moments; they are not things you are likely to desire unless, of course, you are to be considered a pervert of some sort, a masochist. Pain is nobody's friend, my people say. Dealing with more than common, day to day challenges is even less desirable. In the category of the more than ordinary challenges are things like divorce, bereavement, loss of employment, or any other significant disappointment. Devastation describes the feeling of most people when thrust in such circumstances.

Yet, whether nice or not, difficulties and challenges are a part of life and are inevitable. But that they are inevitable in no way makes them nice, you can be sure of that. Difficulties never become desirable, never. What I am pointing out, which is the central thrust of this book, is that difficulties need not maim you; that you need to raise the curtain and see beyond the gloom; that we must not allow difficulties to handicap us; that beyond challenges, there is life; that at the end of the tunnel gloom there is light. Rabbi Jonathan Sacks puts it well: "No one worth admiring ever succeeded without many failures on the way.... If you lack the courage to fail, then you lack the courage to succeed." The idea is thus, that from low moments we can rise and *glow*. I am hesitant about saying rise and *shine* because gloom and really low moments do temper; they modify us to such sobriety that our *shining* after they occur is best described as glow.

A lot stems from this perception and seeing challenges as opportunities can create change(s). This awareness can provide the opportunity for you to think of alternatives to a situation that otherwise looks like a dead end. It makes sense here too what William Barclay in one of his luminous bible commentaries says: that to save someone, you have to believe in their ability to be saved. Applied at the personal level, this pointer can also mean that if you do not prime yourself with the faith that you can overcome or that there is a way out, you will not even recognize the way out if it comes. And sometimes, the alternative that presents itself can lead to even better prospects than the point at which the devastation caught up with you.

Challenges, difficulties and frustrations thus become opportunities for growth, chances for you to prospect for alternatives, other ways to achieve your goal. They are signals pointing at different things you can do, alternative routes and endeavors.

Winston Churchill it was who said, "Never waste a good crisis". He said so at the end of the Second World War, a time when circumstances convened to form the United Nations. Without the unimaginable challenges of the Second World War, this formation would not have been conceivable. Difficulties and setbacks no doubt present opportunities to do even the unimaginable and things that are considered undoable.

All this perhaps does not touch base until the personal element comes in. It is the personal pinch that uplifts any claim to the level of authenticity and utility by being practical, reasonable and doable. And since this book has to be referenced for genuineness, personal experiences come in to bolster and align with the theoretical, philosophical or other choice perspectives herein recommended for you. Thus proposed here is stubborn resilience that is bolstered by help from experientially potent sources, including but not limited to experts, family and the divine. But before the details start coming, here is a beautiful sourced prayer that exemplifies the need for glow no matter the threat to peace.

May I not lose my optimism,
even though the future that awaits me may not be so happy.

May I not lose the will to live,
even though life is often painful.

May I not lose the desire to have great friends,
even knowing that, with the turns that the world takes,
they end up leaving our lives.

That I don't lose the desire to help people,
even though I know that many are unable to see, recognize and repay this aid.

May I not lose my balance,
even though I know that many forces want me to fall.

Let me not lose the light and the gleam in my eyes,
even though I know that many things that I will see in the world will darken my eyes.

May I not lose heart,
even knowing that defeat and loss are two dangerous opponents.

May I not lose my mind,
even though life's temptations are many and delicious.
May I not lose my strong hug,
even though I know that one day my arms will be weak.

May I not lose the beauty and the joy of living,
even though I know that many tears will spring from my eyes and run through my soul.

May I not lose my love for my family,
even though they will often require incredible effort to maintain harmony.

May I not lose the desire to donate this enormous love that exists in my heart, even though I know that it will often be refused.

That I don't lose the desire to be big,
even though the world is small.

And above all, may I never forget that God loves me infinitely!

* * *

I did not need to be loaded with age and experience for the challenge to rock my boat. Mine came just after my Master of Science degree when I enrolled in and started a Ph.D. Program. St. Mary Hospital, Imperial college, University of London was my school of anchor and all was smooth somewhat for the first year. The dreams were soaring; success could not have been doubted for the course was well within my passion and mental reaches.

At the least expected moment, I was diagnosed with what doctors thought was cancer. I spare you the hassled details. Simply, I was informed that the thing was growing at an alarming rate; that I needed urgent surgery. I was twenty-four years old, that age when the skies are only the starting point of expectations and ambitions. It is also the age that has nothing by way of a backup of stored wisdom to tap on. It is an age of speed, but not of stability. Tempest-tossed I succumbed to near-despair. The future became shambles right before my embarrassed eyes.

I resorted to prayer, a force I had been groomed into by my mother and some family relations. With that I settled into hope for the best. Hoping against hope, you could say, I took the only open course and underwent the required surgery. Wonder of wonders, the pathology was benign. The only flickering ray of hope turned out to be the direct beam of saving light.

The lesson I learnt was that it is never really totally dark; absolutely devastating; it never crumbles into such tiny pieces as to eliminate all traces of the destroyed pattern. A ray of hope there is that always goes slow, loiters or lingers, perhaps dismally clad in rags that cloud the brightness of the eventually wonderful outcome. It wouldn't be amiss to recommend that we always look round for that ray because it lightens the dark and the burden of sad times. Indeed, it seems to be the normal way with nature; there is always a contrary vein, some stubbornly contradictory sign against the odds, an anomaly in the trend. This is something which our proclivity for bleak expectations make us notice this more in good times; at such times, we note the dangers that harass our good times, *the sand in our garri*, as the Cameroonian proverbial paints it. We should equally throw calculated side glances at challenging moments in order to spot out the instants of illumination. Simply, we should raise our consciousness about the connectedness of crises and of goodies, as well as their contraries.

One crisis connects with another, which is why the brilliant ray of joy at the benignity of the growth in my body did not altogether cover the trail of mishap. I recovered from the surgery perfectly, but the new hitch was that I could no longer continue the PhD program because new issues arose with the funding. The confounding lull influenced me to understand that it was a time to step right back and squint in a panoramic manner. What direction did I want my life to take? Was I to insist on continuing the PhD or was I to choose another avenue?

Somewhere in my readings in psychology I had read that we mostly end up choosing our second best. This might be debatable, but perhaps the fact that many people are not totally satisfied with their choices bolsters that projection.

There was one other choice desirable for me— the choice to switch to the school of medicine. I had nursed the desire to read medicine and now it was obvious that the burning desire was not gone away yet. In fact, it had been a matter of serious thought when I graduated with my first degree and an alternative to the PhD after my Master's degree. The constraints had been money.

The interruption in my PhD program at the University of London became a beckoning opportunity to make progress in the direction of medicine. Medicine would take me where I had wanted to be. The decision was made. To medical school I decided to go, but the rumbling question came with it—what was I to do differently or needed to do differently to mark out the choice? Then, too, came a long and deep look at the education and cost of living in both the United Kingdom and United States of America, with questions of financial prospects and their sustainability.

Conclusion: the United States was the place to go; not an easy option, though. Logistics, travel, application details and relocation hazards all came in congested tangles to be loosed. The road was predictably windy but the double choice of medicine and the US was definitive.

How to get to the US, the challenges in the process and at the journey's end all came jostling and asking me to face them in their crudity. Those were the practical part, the realities, which until now were a notional choice I had made. The steps proved slower than the pat decision. I went on to an investigation of the American educational system. There, a steep wall robustly stood up to me, blinding my vision—it was impossible for me to apply directly to medical school, my not having done premed being a stolid concern. Securing an interview too was impossible.

I needed no marabout to investigate the obvious truth that my journey to become a medical doctor had to be arduous, long, and maybe dispiriting. While those were facts I couldn't change, the power to handle them was not far to seek: acceptance and mental preparedness. It was but a journey and that was the pack I needed, an identification badge, so to say. With these all obstacles to be encountered already met their equal, each like a step at a time.

The intricacy wobbled the details, which soon shone out in the need to start by going to a graduate school. It was a signaled long road to freedom and I could guess that rightly. Yes, the steep cliff can always be climbed, surmounted. The difficult task could always be done. All you needed was the will to conquer, the patience to take the long road while having the perennial mental presence to continue in focus even when a detour is necessitated. All that took time, but then, time was always at hand and time was not only the leveler of human ups and downs, differences and dread; it was the meeting point of distant ends.

The far fling of time's stretch while I carried on with grad studies brought with it certain consolations, certain advantages, while I weighed the processes of getting into medical school. In the grad studies, I wanted to continue with medical microbiology, particularly to do research in HIV and AIDS.

The excellent maneuvering, which patience and focus provided, was not enough to take care of everything, certainly not the financial pinch. The basics were living expenses and school fees. To this I had the onus of deciding where, in the vast American country with myriads of opportunities, I was going to attend school.

Communication technology was still creeping at that time; there was yet no internet then in common use. Painstakingly, I inched my way into and across the Peterson's guide to direct me. I went through it, copied the names of many schools and reviewed each of their Medical Microbiology departments. From this close look, I noted the schools that were offering research in HIV and AIDS. To each of these I then wrote a personally crafted letter directed at their principal investigators.

I was honest about my situation. I wanted to study for a PhD focused on HIV and AIDS and detailed that I could not financially sustain myself. I would appreciate any form of financial assistance through the program and would work for it, I begged and offered at the same time. I hadn't learnt of the various kinds of begging, but self-esteem and dignity made up for my ignorance. The picture I gave of myself in the manner I begged was of someone only temporarily indigent but in the prospect of rising above the wretchedness in due course. Hope floated above all the misery suggested by my penury.

The gentle personal letter to the individual investigators concealed the fiery push behind the project. None of the investigators perhaps was privy to the fact that my attached curriculum vitae and letter ratatated in machine gun fashion, enough to multiply kill. I was not to miss any possible point of penetration as I spewed and launched piles and piles of these application packages. Counting gets lost, but I mailed more than fifty of these to the United States before sitting back to watch and await the playback of my assaults.

Some kindly people graciously responded to my letter, explaining that, while they would be happy to have me in their program, it was not feasible to assist me financially. Some did not bother to respond, but the response 'no' overfilled my mailbox. So, literally, nothing was forthcoming. To relieve the tension of expectancy pulled to tearing point by doubt, I went away for a few days to be with my aunt.

The breakoff was necessary because what awaited me needed deep breathing before a takeoff. Well, I returned to my hostel, not very expectant, given the nay messages that had become the constant in my agitated posture of anticipation. A message was waiting for me. It was from a certain Dr. Gendelman, a name I easily associated with the idea of a *gentleman* and its entailment. In fact, the 'd' that replaced the medial 't' only softened, i.e. softly modified the edges of the pronunciation, putting a downy feel to it. All this I took in in one quick recce. There was something positive even about the name, I decided. He had called from the United States and wanted me to call him back.

When I looked over my correspondences, I realized that he was one of the people I had sent a letter to. That is what then pricked my attention and then a jittery excitation followed. For some reason, I paused and decided to call the next day. Sheer instinct or observation informed my inner response system that important calls should be made in the morning hours of work time. That is an apt time for scheduling further and later ad hoc meetings and follow-ups for the day.

Armed with this practical and almost cultural view of calling time, I dialed Dr Gendelman's office. It was his secretary, Karen, who picked up the phone. Dr Gendelman had travelled but would be back in three days; he was sure going to call me, she assured. Short as it was, that conversation was the first positive note and I have not forgotten the thrill it left in me, so reassuring. I stayed put in my room on the third day, all expectation.

True as a clock, my phone rang. I picked it up. The voice at the other end of the line said,

"Good morning; can I speak to Adeline?"

My heart missed several beats and rose in tempo but I managed to say something in response:

"Speaking; this is she..."

"I am Dr. Howard Gendelman. How are you?"

My heart still in my mouth, I answered, "I am fine, thank you."

As often happens, the start is the odd point. Before long, the conversation was flowing and defining the journey I would embark on to lead me where I am today. Dr. Gendelman explained the nature of his research in HIV/AIDS. He had faculty positions at Creighton University (CU) and the University of Nebraska Medical Center (UNMC). The deadline for submission of application for postgraduate studies at UNMC had passed. There was one week left for CU, he said and if I wanted to come to the US, I should submit my application right away.

I jumped to the opportunity. I was serious and was starting the application process as soon as the telephone conversation ended. I was all over with gratitude for the opportunity he was willing to give me.

When I hung up the phone, I went dumb. Excitement was in my pulse. I lost no time in calling the admissions office at Creighton University for required details. The next week was hectic, completing the application and obtaining the supporting documents being the tenor of everything I carried out. The excitement used up itself and calm returned for me to patiently await the decision of the admission committee.

It was only notionally a gamble because with the go ahead of Dr Gendelman, the rest depended on whether I followed the right formalities. And sure enough, before long, a mail came from Creighton University. No matter how confident I had been before now, I trembled violently as I opened the envelope. My eyes shot for the most significant point in the mail: I had been accepted into the Graduate program to pursue a Doctor of Philosophy (Ph.D.) degree in Medical Microbiology. I was also awarded a tuition remission.

Pent-up emotions burst forth in rapid tears that ran down my cheeks. I was overwhelmed. From the deepest recesses of my being, inexpressible gratitude to God welled up. I was thankful for Dr. Gendelman, truly grateful to him. Immediately I rang him up to share the good news with him. He was happy for me and said he looked forward to working with me. And since goodies come in bundles, he had a new additional joy to punch in. He told me he had a grant that would cover some stipend for me. God of wonders, how you work! What news!

I had family in the United States, but they were mostly in the East coast, so there was no family cushioning to expect. I made all the arrangements and in August 1994, I set out for Omaha, Nebraska, in the Midwest, having no more than $1000 in the world to start life with. Dr. Floyd Knoop, the program director at CU, arranged for me to be picked up at the airport by Ms Vonetta Byington. She worked in the department and that was the start of a lasting friendship bond.

I spent my first week in a motel and with the help of Dr. Knoop, I got accommodation from where I could easily access school. It was a wise prioritizing, which limited my choices, especially as I could not afford a car. Before long, it was clear that the best option was to live on campus.

The graduate student housing was a reasonable

distance off campus, but the university shuttle transported students to and from campus. The housing was full, however. Dr. Knoop and Vonetta continued inquiring. Then they spotted a place at the freshman dormitory on campus but wondered how I would take it. When the information reached me, however, it was sheer delight. It was to me a welcome, nay, golden opportunity. So, after one week of living in a motel, I moved in to share a room with a freshman.

All this was preliminary, for until now I had not met the man whose supportive hints led me to apply and be admitted to this college— Dr. Gendelman.

* * *

Not much happens in institutionalized setups that can go up for individual or societal news of any note. I did have a personal and private news-worthy happening, however. This happened in my second week in Omaha and was plainly the experience of encounter with Dr. Gendelman. I have already indicated how his name struck me as emblematic of gentlemanliness with all the entailment. Now I was going to meet him face to face. The gentility embedded in his name was introduced by his coming to pick me up for lunch. He fitted my first hunch, a gentle spirit with a warmly welcoming smile.

When he told me, "Just call me Howie; everybody calls me Howie," he was sure expanding and blending gentility with humility and authenticity, which is the complex also known as integrity. I took it the way it came, but must confess that I missed the gentility embedded in the name *Gendelman*. I guess goodies do not always announce their worth by name. Some do though, like sugarcane and perhaps lemonade. But some names are just names and we just have to learn to associate them with the goodies or other qualities we deem fit. I often wonder what part of the word *honey* stores the sweetness, or the word *gold* keeps the wealth-worth weight. Silver may well be called silly or ruby be robe or grub; the sound does not always echo the sense, which is why when it does, the literati of literature make so much of and give it an impossible name—*onomatopoeia*—whatever the connection between the long name might be with a twit, tweet, cackle or gargle, for example.

Well, Howie took me to downtown Omaha for lunch at an Italian restaurant. He was magnanimous and dainty, without being finicky and we talked at length over lunch. You sensed kindheartedness in his every word, gesture and aspiration. You felt the presence of a focused person exuding that inner grit that generates purposefulness even to the passive.

In so many words and ways he communicated to me that hard work pays off. At least, that is something I registered as an understood thing he was emphasizing.

Lunch was soon over, a brief but memorable time spent in the presence of an inspiring professional. He drove me back to campus after lunch, came out of the car and pointing up, caught his aspirations for me in a simple one-liner. He said to me, "Look up there."

I stared into the blue and white clouds, wondering what monstrosity or apparition inspired that command. That is when he came down with the hammer on the nail:

"As long as you work hard, the sky is the limit." He then added that he would see me in the second semester, when I was scheduled to start research in his laboratory. That was that and I returned to my room, Howie's words, for all their simplicity and commonplace feel, resonating with my deepest views. Those words have since been the perpetual fire and fuel for my aspirations and execution.

Talk of first impressions, even by mail; talk of the first impression made by the overtones in the name Gendelman: my first impression was right. Howie remains a selfless person who believes in assisting and giving opportunities to other people. Even after I graduated with a doctorate and moved on, he has continued as my silent mentor.

Okay, I obtained my Ph.D., a milestone of academic achievement for sure. But neither rest nor the envisaged comfort came as a matter of course. I would later read of St Augustine's prayerful dictum: 'Our hearts are made for thee, o Lord, and restless till they rest in thee.'

In the meantime, I was in the restless state, really restlessly, for I wanted to work in the industry for about two years before furthering my education. I applied for two jobs and attended the interviews but did not get the positions. Disappointment started rubbing away my emotions; time was passing by and I needed to pay my bills. Thankfully, it never gets totally impenetrably dark—a pet notion I have come to hold with great conviction. A starlet, a flicker of fire, a gentle glow or some such factor always mollifies the bite of bitterness, the acuity of the stench, the gloom pitch of the dark or desperate circumstance. It is up to us to watch out for that flicker.

Fairly soon, I took a position that paid me just about twice what I was making as a doctoral student—not much to write home about, you could say. It was a post-doctoral position at Creighton University. For, although my research there was in Microbiology, it was not on HIV and AIDS. The British have it that sometimes you have to eat humble pie. Here was humble pie for me and I had no elbow space for any form of an alternative or choice. I took the job. Truly humble pie it turned out to be and generated daily disappointment for me. It was frustrating to be where you never planned or envisaged you should be, to be in such a place not by true choice in which genuine alternatives are available but by circumstantial coercion as it were.

I went to work but was not happy where I spent at least one third of each day. Going to work every day was a challenge. Without a doubt, there are and should be a thousand ways out or (for that matter) in to such frustrating circumstances. One of them, I learnt later, was proposed by John Keats, the British poet of the early twentieth century. He suggested what he summed as *negative capability*, i.e., the ability to stay afloat in an unsteady circumstance. You keep the fort against an onslaught of bludgeoning ravages, knowing that that instant of the storm is a process that deserves its place in your life.

Well, I was not yet into that philosophical stance; restiveness in the unpleasant circumstance was my natural turn of mind. I was facing it instead of flowing with it pro tem. True to that confrontation, I sat up and gave my circumstances a detailed analytical frilling. It was not my ideal job or place to be, I owned. I needed no magician to tell me that; my daily sad going to and return from work were bright enough even for the visually challenged. I went to it unhappy every morning and looked forward to weekends as best days because I did not have to be at the dissatisfying job.

What alternatives did I have? I thought of medical school, how I had wanted to work in industry, gearing up on working towards medical school. But there were gaps to fill which I hadn't yet filled. Not having done my undergraduate degree in the US, but in England, I suffered the deficiency of entering a new system midway. The British system of education, structured differently, had a more specialized undergraduate curriculum. My having obtained a BSc focused on Microbiology, coupled with some science classes, didn't provide me with enough material for the medical school admission test (MCAT). Worse was that, whatever classes I had taken earlier, those were evidently so many years behind me. The knowledge gathered was ensconced in the long term memory, needing some form of sparking in order to come up handy for the present. Much new learning too was required for me to succeed in the MCAT.

Was I making the most of my circumstances? Sometimes we are blinded by watching at the limitations and missing on the opportunities. I had to open wide my eyes to notice and make effective use of one of the benefits of being on the staff of Creighton University: if your boss could attest that attending two courses (which would be tuition free) wouldn't interfere with your job function, you could go right ahead and pursue your courses. For as little as requesting it, I got my boss's letter of approval to enroll for the courses. I guess this ability to sort out opportunities in painful circumstances is an aspect of resilience. It surely helps to enliven the spirit with a refocusing freshness.

That then is how I came to register and start premed classes in the evening, taking two every semester. I would work during the day, take classes in the evening and go home to do whatever homework had to be done. With these too went reading up on my research and designing experiments. Each day was packaged in suffocating and tiring work. Embrace it I did and rolled on fairly stoically.

The gritty embrace of these duty labors was by no means leisurely or pleasant in the light of being facile. But I was not stinting the intensity of my engagement. The cross would be heavier and less manageable for anyone who chose to make it drag on the ground instead of a committed uplifting of the load from the ground and a courageous march forward. Most times, burdens are made more difficult to carry because we go about the loads without commitment, without will. I was only now embracing with insightful practice this lesson which I had merely notionally understood.

Before, I knew it, I had finished my premed classes, all tuition free. Hope was rising and a lighter air blew at my face with gentle caress as I enrolled and took the MCAT. I next applied to medical school even earlier than I had projected. So, working at Creighton, despite the tediousness, became an opportunity. You could say that the drawn-out way in which the challenges of my working at the university were evolved tended to hide the fact that they were just as brittle and subject to modification by attitudinal dispositions as the less drawn-out challenges. It was a hard lesson fraught with guesswork and experimental uncertainty. Yet, the lesson did register itself as a take-home.

CHAPTER TWO

MAKING GOOD THE BAD

Plan – a Primer

Converting difficulties to edification, bad to good, is an engineering endeavour. It is a deliberate action, the forging of circumstances and events so as to transform challenges into rewards and step up from low to high and glad from sad. You decide, strategize and meticulously carry out action so as to bring about a particular and desired effect. In the process, there is great value in combining a plan of action with positive thinking; redirecting the course of an otherwise negative, bad, or challenging event needs several composite moves. But first comes the need for you to decide and then to take action that should be moderated by the right attitude.

Primary then is the need for you to make up your mind that you will move beyond whatever situation presents itself. In the last chapter I referred to William Barclay's comment that you cannot save a people you do not believe in. This stated condition also fits the self and its prospects: You cannot move forward if you don't decide to do so. It is in the mind. In the mind is where the propellant is lodged and deciding to move beyond limitations, whatever they be, is the mother resolution.

From the above key move, action can now follow. And action in this respect is a composite of physical, psychological and spiritual inputs. Each of these inputs needs the staying power of the right frame of mind, the attitude, to stimulate and maintain the right thought processes. In other words, anticipating success is the step forward in overcoming barriers. But decision, action and attitude are the unified trio, the squad that makes and ensures end success.

Make a Decision

The mother step of steps in the right direction is a practical decision. In this respect, I would like to paraphrase "Self-reliance", a fable retold by Patrick Tata *Twenty-four Fables* published by Emengu Int'l. It bolsters the idea of the power of decisiveness.

Accordingly, a field full of sparrows anticipated harvest time to end their spell of plenty. In wait, the winged fellows kept their ears on the ground for telltale signs of the appropriate stage to get going. For one thing, change wasn't considered right when not indicated by circumstantial imperatives; for when it is not necessary to change, it is necessary *not* to change. That is a thing which the winged fellows had heard; they indeed liked the tinkle in the parallelism.

As the story went, one young sparrow did overhear the farm owner lamely relate to others that he was going to invite some people to help him do the harvest. Fear-stricken, the young sparrow rushed to relate the news to wise old father sparrow. The fledgling had not the discriminating faculty to hear what has not been said just from the tone in the voice of what is actually said.

Old wise father sparrow knew each thing unsaid and saw the invisible from the actions on display for normal eyes. To the fledgling he calmly said that there was nothing to bother about just yet. With birdlike faith in the wisdom of its old dad, the young sparrow returned to days of plenty; he fell back on field days of leisure and open-door meals. Excited tweets of sheer delight spun webs around the ethereal songs which the winds of the field helped to harmonize with a swishing babble of fluty voices.

Meanwhile, in the youngster's head there rang with echoing rebounds the quaint remark which dad had underscored:

"The man who only relies on others is not in a hurry to get things done just yet," old father sparrow had explained.

When, next the farmer visited and said he was going to hire laborers to do the harvest with him, old father sparrow in a near-panic-rushed voice called out to all the distractions of busy bevies of sparrows:

"It's time to move, folks! When someone takes a

decision to act instead of shillyshallying, such a one indeed means business."

* * *

Slightly different, but corroborative too is the story of Ms CG who now owns and runs a billing company, success all in it with glamor. The rise to that success started with the really down moment when she lost her job, a devastating low. Anxiety overspread and shadowed her every thought, word and deed. An hour in her office listening to her was exposure to a deluge of woes that preceded the start of her company.

Finding a new job was difficult, she said. So she had a mind to start her own business. But a personal business was not going to materialize just from an intention. So it was not simply a given—not just yet, for having in mind is like having a wish and not like making a decision. The challenges were still nebulous in her conception, formless and difficult to manage. The assumption was that it was going to be so hard and difficult and tough and ...impossible. And impossible it should be until a definitive step is decided upon.

By and by, it came to be. It didn't come easy and it came in a darker moment, perhaps to bolster the proverbial that the darkest hour announces dawn. That is how the day came when she became terribly distraught, pushed to the wall of fight-back-or-be-crushed. She hadn't heard the song of John Minang about fighting back when you got bushed to the wall, but wisdom is universal and she certainly tapped it from the same common ocean of solutions.

That dark moment, she knew she had to decide. And she did. Once the mind settled on her course, the rest was procedural. She did everything it took to start her own billing company. Taking the bull by the horn, as the saying goes, deciding on the way forward, nearly always leads to greater and better achievements. Today she is a successful businesswoman, doing billing and credentialing for multiple medical practices.

When I listened to Ms CG, I read into my friend's situation, the turmoil in her mind with all the woolly conjectures and how these all were dispersed by one stroke of the mind—decision. That is when I engraved it in gold in my mind and meant to spread it out as I am doing now—*make a decision*.

Dillydallying, floating like aimless clouds, flowing with the currents of no purpose, being washed by rainwater or bashed at the curves and banks of stream currents of wasting water—that's just what sources our woes, especially in situations of crises. The best of us decide on action *sometimes* and are glad we did or perhaps judge that we could have done better, which is just okay. I had made many decisions in my life; indeed, who hasn't? But now I realized I too had missed out on some opportunities because I kept postponing deciding. The book you are now reading is an example. I kept pushing it forward, procrastinated finishing it. I found it troubling to decide that it was possible for me to create enough time for it. One excuse tumbled on another. But then, when I made up my mind, when I decided that I would not procrastinate anymore, I saw changes; I made time to write and the rest fitted in like a *T* with opportunities converging to make just everything work for the goal.

Make a decision—just three words; if you but take the call and stick to it, much starts falling into place. For when there is action, all corollaries spin and spiral into more action and greater successes. That way, transformations of even unconnected lines of thought come to bolster the action, changing the course of life. The painful becomes endurable and the good becomes better as better steps up to best with that one stroke—decision.

It is a tricky thing to decide, though, and there are minutiae that might require adjustments for particular decisions to be taken. But at bottom, making up one's mind, deciding on a line of action, that *is* a big help. Decide that the challenge or difficulty you are going through will not maim and sure enough it wouldn't.

On the other hand, if you decide to wallow in the misery you are flung in by unwieldy winds; if you just let things be, allowing yourself to be knocked about by life— you are in for fulltime low and lower days, years and a life time of self-defeat from deadening knocks.

Even at the risk belaboring the point ad nauseam, I would say it over and over again: *make a decision*. With decision, the key clicks open to a floodgate of opportunities. For when you decide, you will better identify the goal, set your eyes on the ball, find just where to put your best efforts and resources into attaining that goal. When you decide, the right mindset is energized; opportunities start rolling before, literally tumbling over each other in fostering your goal. Indeed, your decision gives a compass into which breakthroughs come to flood your aspirations. Your eyes too get opened to see opportunities in circumstances and situations you would not have seen otherwise.

The importance of a decision so clearly enunciated begs question: when should that decision be taken? It does not really matter at what stage you take the decision to move on. It is always a step forward, a step that often deletes fear. And in so saying, I am minded of the fact that fear is the crossroads of hope and doubt, the dangling in-between spot of shivering motives. A decision, even a negative one, breaks the skeletal bones of fear, which is a negative emotion that totes with it correlative and far-reaching effects.

Make a decision! Let that imperative statement ring with its numerous advantages. I have heard it said in other words, "just do it". But that coinage seems to lack the moral choice and deliberation hosted by the one we are saying and resaying. For a decision presupposes calculation, pros and cons considerations and a moral preference. It is thrust with reasonableness and responsibility. As far as you are concerned, put two and two together faster and then step forward. When this happens, not only do you find that you have overcome the threatening difficulty, but that you physically overcome concurrently with your changed mentality. Then you start floating above challenges and your constitution lives in great freedom, a freedom that sees everything as possible to you, because of your faith which propels and guides your disposition. That is how the rise from low to glow happens. Low moments engender gloom; the decision to rise from it is a choice to transform from that gloom to glow.

Mindset change is, by default, an arduous thing. But when concrete action shows what can be achieved by even a single difficult decision, a certain understanding lubricates the mind's ways. Noticeably, the mind starts naturally to propend to positive perspectives. You can be sure that sometimes it takes great effort to change mentality from negative to positive. This is even more so if the person has shuffled through or come across difficulty after difficulty, challenge after challenge and unsuccessful attempt after unsuccessful attempt. Every bit of effort helps. For when you decide to move beyond difficulties, somehow, that goal gets imprinted in your mind and determines its natural tendency—self-realization. The mind is such a powerful tool that once it decides on a thing, it does everything by moving all your faculties and circumstances to achieve that goal.

The Power of Positive Thinking by Norman Vincent Pearle is a book which I read in adolescence. I still remember it to this day. Of recent I have come to realize how the principles outlined by Pearle sync with biblical thought and, perhaps, with all the literature of other successful lifestyles. Those who read the bible might remember that in Matthew 9:29 it reads, "According to your faith will it be done to you." This sounds so simplistic and at the same time arcane. In a rather casual manner, the expression introduces us to the impact of mind and attitude to a person's reality or experience.

Allowing for the simplicity, let us blindly take it on grounds of the fact that great things are not necessarily far to seek. And here perhaps we have things like the vital oxygen we need, the water we need and even the earth on which we stand. Let us, even if for no other reason than that, make sure not to underestimate the power of the mind.

The simple example in my case is the decision to write this book, which I have already broached. The power of the mind came to the fore once I decided to stop procrastinating about writing it. On the instant, a whole chained lot of transformation took place. I visualized the various positive impacts which my writing would bring about on the lives of others. That encouraged me further. To that encouragement was added every stride, big or small that I made. Eventually, through multiple processes, I have reached the end and here is the book you are reading.

Do I give the impression that you wave a magic wand and then all happens? That is not what I mean. It would be misleading, nay, false, to give the impression that the mental change freezes all challenges. It does not. The decision to forge on does not remove the sharp asphalt, the kinky curves, the steep climb or the interference of other traffic on the way. The decision to forge on does not stop or swipe off the rough realities of the road. What it does: It assures you that the rough road leads to a desired goal; that, despite the sharp bends and breath-debilitating gradients and interfering traffic with stuffily polluted airs, the road yet leads to a desired end— the decided goal.

As to the writing process, I wrote down as often as useful snippets came to my mind. But there were days when I felt empty and low with discouragement. On such days, I took refuge in and consoled myself by looking at what had been penned down on fruitful days. So previous writing became fuel for dry days. Some days, even doing so was not coming easy. But, overall, I wouldn't let that deter me. The lesson is simply that temporary dryness or challenges must not be allowed to rob us of the focus at reaching our goals.

Set a Goal

You do not have a goal if you have not set any. At the risk of sounding repetitive and even circumlocutious, let me state it that it is important to set goals. If you do not set a goal, you will not have an idea where you are going. A goal is the foundation; it is the object, the pulling point and direction to go. Set your eyes upon the goal and your feet upon the path to that goal. Once the goal is set, it orientates thinking, movement and other processes. A goal automatically gives you an opportunity to think of where you want to be, what you want to achieve. All you have in hand or come across, active and passive factors, amazingly diverse resources, all start pooling in to enable you to reach that target.

The goal is a vision you work towards. It adjusts your movement by offering specific objectives to direct your actions and interpretations of your setup. This includes even unthinkable objects or resources. A plate, hammer, drying line, etc. each is designed for a specific use. But when an objective is created, these diverse objects designed for different uses can be brought to advance a new objective. Supposing a thief invaded your home and you had to defend yourself; if you had enough mental presence, you would weaponize the plate, hammer or drying line to defend home or self. That is how a goal makes every available situation serve your purpose. The urgency of the goal, vision or objective cuts off distraction, enabling you to avoid wasting time and to work smart.

Of course, this rather rosy picture is valid when you look at the whole picture. While you prosecute the course, while you tread the path, while you bend your back to drudging, back-twisting labor, you then simultaneously realize how lofty, satisfying and self-fulfilling it actually is. Fulfillment comes at the end, though. Do not therefore be overly concerned if things do not work exactly the way you plan. A little wobble does not shatter the essence.

It is in fact very okay to, within good reasons, re-visit

and re-adjust your goal and refocus the process. It is the aspect of accountability you are working at. For a goal engenders accountability. It not only has specifics by which you measure your behavior, but it enables you to be accountable to yourself. You might, as part of that accountability, draw up timelines for various tiers of achievement to be reached. This calls for prudence because you will need to shrewdly judge the extent to which set goals or timelines are achievable.

An over-ambitious program of activities and mini-goals to be achieved could crash the whole process. Good measure requires good knowledge of the self and of available resources. That knowledge allows you to anticipate your achievements, measure your progress and use the positive end attainment as a booster to happy living. For life is lived in the moment but nourished by the future we aim at.

It is then obvious that goal setting ends procrastination. It triggers goal-oriented behavior along with its positive effects. It dynamizes purposeful action and self-motivation, having the effect of raising our morale, enhancing self-confidence. With increased faith in the self, the goal-oriented individual's productivity is greatly increased. What a trigger! This simply elevates the push factor and sublimates your living, enabling you to be the best version of yourself, the best you possible.

Start Smart Small

The glowing picture of the grand finale, the ambitious world-record-breaking euphoria—that has to be tempered by caution. Do not bite more than you can chew. A gentle process of training is necessary. Start with small goals. Awe-inspiring goals are good only if they are within achievement range. It is disheartening and counterproductive to aspire to goals which you will not be able to achieve within the time limit you set. If you are in a situation that is rather too difficult, if you are down and out, failing to meet your objective might just plunge you into greater discouragement, which is not good for the journey at all.

It is advisable therefore to set small, more obviously achievable goals and to use each mini goal as scaffolding for greater reaches. Nothing succeeds like success, they say, and failure often engenders more failure. One success sets you on the path of successive successes. It is something quite impressed in nature where, for example, the infant doesn't normally skip the stage but must crawl before going on to walk and run.

Each success level needs applause and or reward, no matter how small. Each end point is the beginning of a new journey to a little higher level. The reward should perhaps only be symbolic. It could be as simple as patting yourself on the back and saying, "I did it. This is something I could never have thought possible." From this, you can add one aspirant tendency immediately. If I can with a little persistence achieve this, then I can certainly achieve more by taking up the next challenge. In this spirit, the next challenge is approached with a strong sense of purpose and achievement confidence.

That is the advantage of setting successively achievable goals, mini goals, so to say. On the set small goals is built other goals, each goal achieved, becoming a staircase leading to greater heights. It is recommended for the beginner as for the guru that writing down the intended goals provides visual reminders, keeping them on track. The written goal can be parsed for progress markers. Your progress should then be visited and assessed.

Where you have reached in the goal achieving process spurs you to move on. So, although small goals are desirable, they are only small for smart engagement. The ultimate is the grand finale, but the mini goals are units of the great goal grand plan, a kind of serialized ranking of the same edifice. It's very much like the man who draws a plan to build a mansion but partitions his work into smaller units which in his mind are each complete— the foundation with complete budgeting and time frame; the walls come connected but only discretely to the foundation. They have their own budgeting, timing and execution details. The same goes for the roofing and for finishing fittings such as electricity, water, plastering, and floor tiling. It must be remembered, however, that each goal achievement point is only reached by action, a thing requiring proper orientation and follow up.

Action

Blandly put, action is important. It determines the kind of outcome of a situation, being a corollary of goal setting and the processes towards achievement. Making a decision is one thing; knowing where you want to go is another. But decision and direction are only starting points. The gritty part is the work on the ground, the action taken. So, once a thought or an idea is born, and the processes outlined, you have to act, and it is action that brings strategy into fruition. An idea or a thought not put into action is only as good as a mere whim or passing thought. Thought is like a seed you have in hand—not yet sown and watered to sprout.... Commonsense tells us that propagating the seed requires a lot more than keeping it in hand. You need to sow, water, manure, weed, protect, and spray against disease. You need to nurture the seed for it to grow. That is where action comes in. The dainty hand that is sleek from non-action is irrelevant here. The skilled and tough hand—that is what is needed.

So after establishing your goal and developing a road map on how to get there, the grit is to trudge. That, to many, is the reality point. Until action is initiated, passionately embraced, all else is shadowy, a passing wind that lacks substance. Goal and strategy are "the where" and "the how" as principles, including "the when" and "by what means". They are achieved by "the doing", action.

Among the obstacles to action, fear sticks out. Fear

of the unknown, fear of failure, fear of fear itself...these hold back a lot of fruitful action. Even among successful people, failure in some ventures is but normal. What they do not let happen is for fear of such occasional failure to hold them back. Fear should be integrated as a mere process issue, a slight hitch best ignored.

Really, fear is made up of two things: hope of success and countered by doubt. If you suppress doubt, fear dies to hope. If you raise the level of faith, fear dies to faith. If you trust the dream too, or light up the goal, or pull the vision closer to sight and forge on to reach the purposed end, fear cows from view; fear hides, disappears.

Do not, therefore, let fear of failure stop you. Do, however, consider some failure as the spicy aspect of life for there is really no life without some failure. Even in young dreams, the pattern is constant. That is why the child learns to sit only after many awkward failing attempts at sitting; learns to crawl after botched, near disastrous attempts. To stand, the child submits to many disgraceful totters, collapses and flat falls. The dangling dithers with many accidents are introductory to firm walk. This natural process of progress is through retrogressive performances, a thing repeated in nearly all spheres of life. Albeit painful, failures are thus a valuably integral part of life.

Action then must overcome fear and go on. No matter the opportunities availed to you, if you do not take concrete advantage of those opportunities by action, nothing comes of the opportunities. It is idiomatic that opportunity comes to the ready and may well be considered nonexistent if the would-be beneficiary is oblivious or unready. In fact, for those who have no obvious opportunities, when they act, they bring about amazing effects. These effects create greater opportunities for them and for those associated with their action.

If you do not take advantage of opportunities, you cannot accomplish what you seek/desire. That is the rule. For no matter how highly hailed you are for certain talents, skills or know-how, these amount to nothing if you do not act on them or with them. No progress can be registered on mere cogitation and strategizing. Intentions color but do not replace action. Thoughts, intentions and strategy, these have to get gritty, be involved with the hard, often harsh or concrete realities on the grounds. There is no way around the fact that action is the route to the next level; nothing more and nothing less.

So, keeping in mind that action is what takes you to the next level in achieving your goal, leave fear behind and act with the conviction that it will work. Faith, action and hope as has been indicated, together and individually confront and overcome fear. In its process, action too defeats fear. But whatever the case, even a single step forward can open floodgates of new opportunities. As these new opportunities blossom, more action leads to even more.

The value of action reminds one of the pop phrase: *Just do it*. It is an imperative that evokes the feel of irresponsibility, sadly. Yet, in it is thrust the strong message that action, rather than standing by like the guilty bystander in Thomas Merton's spirituality, is required for both the world and individuals to progress.

Just do it, attributed to the *Nike* company as a trademark of courage since 1988 has been dramatized by Shia LeBeouf in a motivational presentation worth extracting here:

Do it! Just do it! Don't let your dreams be dreams.
Yesterday, you said, "tomorrow". So, just do it!
Make your dreams come true: just do it!
Some people dream success
while you gona wake up and work harder;
You should get to the point where anyone would quit.
Yes, you can: just do it.
If you're tired of starting over, don't give up
…

The tone of irresponsibility in *Just do it* only has a backing when *doing it* is not directed by a properly rehearsed vision, goal, dream and strategy. As you *do* it, one bold step emboldens the next; one good step uplifts another. As you take each positive step, you are encouraged to another and then another in rapid succession.

Caution must not be thrown to the winds in action, however, for *action, action, action…* is a misleading catchphrase if we take it up without corollaries. Action absolutely needs bolsters, fenders and upshots, one of which is attention to feedback. Feedback, the washback effect of action, should redefine your action or cause you to adjust the parameters of the next action. So, action has to be attended by attitudinal awareness.

Attitude

The importance of how we react to what happens to us cannot be overstressed. This is also known as attitude, which is essentially how we behave due to our feeling or opinion on a thing or person. What happens to us in life *is*, without a doubt, important; but what we make of it is even more important.

Since the catch is usually in the management of difficulties rather than pleasures, it is in place here to examine how we react in adversity. Two broad choices are open to us—the choice to be positive or to be negative. Either of them is behavioral, that is, attitudinal.

FIG 1. The Positive Cylinder

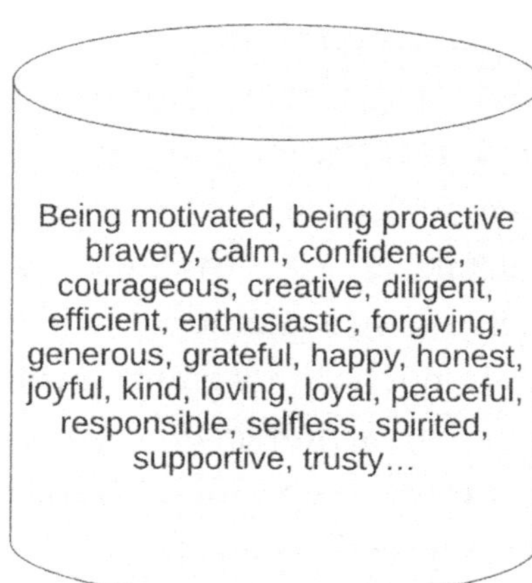

Being motivated, being proactive
bravery, calm, confidence,
courageous, creative, diligent,
efficient, enthusiastic, forgiving,
generous, grateful, happy, honest,
joyful, kind, loving, loyal, peaceful,
responsible, selfless, spirited,
supportive, trusty...

FIG 2. The Negative Chart

Anger, anxiousness, arrogance, complaint, despair, dishonesty, egocentrism, fakeness, falsity, fear, greed, hatred, hopelessness, ignorance, impatience, inauthenticity, indecisiveness, indifference, inferiority, insincerity, jealousy, laziness, loneliness, procrastination, regretfulness, sadness, self-centeredness, selfishness, stressfulness, superficiality, tenseness, uncertainty, violence, worry

Each sentiment is tied to our feeling or opinion about what is at stake. For obvious reasons, a positive attitude is the recommended one, and one reason for this is that being positive engenders better results. Different studies in various disciplines highlight the value of positivity such as the preferment of smiling over frowning, of letting go as opposed to bitterness, letting go of anger over being warlike and vindictive. The above charts list some of the emotions in the positive and in the negative classes. A lot more can be added but the underlying fact is that the negative attitudes or emotions are bad winds that bring no good or actually predicate evil while the positive emotions anticipate and predicate good.

The bottom line is that attitudes to events, life and people will influence outcomes. An attitude qualifies and tones an action. Attitude even reverts to thought or mentality, through its relation with feelings and opinion. From that thought level, attitude colors the substance and the quality of our actions. By being the drive behind behavior, attitude determines how you manage failure, opportunities, and even successes. It goes without saying that for this reason it is necessary to guard against an attitude that is defective.

The need for a positive attitude cannot be overemphasized here. In fact, a positive attitude is the de facto default stance recommended. True, self-assertion can sometimes seem to stretch to the edge of the choleric mode, for example. But when that happens, the assertive person should be aware that the positive line has been crossed. And it is not only positive self-assertion that can be abused. Virtually all good things can be abused. For example, gentleness can be so downtrodden as to bring about an end to all firmness for the good. A politeness that is unable to rebuke evil is itself evil. And so, abuse aside, the positive attitude yields a certain situational control that enables the individual to continue in calm and in the right mindset towards their goal.

The negative attitude, often manifested in negative emotions, is like churned water whose stirred bottom mud clouds the whole and dulls visibility. Without visibility, progress is slow or even halted. A positive attitude can be said to be that calm clarity, which enables the individual's mind-set to navigate through challenges or simple realities with a sense of direction. By it, a person can make choices and devise productive action plans towards their vision or goal. A positive attitude keeps the mind's eye clear enough to see opportunities where others see none; to see openings where others only see blocked walls. A positive mindset is linked to the idea of faith in there being a way out of every tangle. Once that faith becomes activated, the individual searches for a way out with the assurance that that way out exists and can be found. His effort is no longer about the reality but about locating that certain reality. The positive person goes with enthusiasm, leaving no stone unturned, being assured of success.

There is no doubt therefore that a positive attitude advances action and the realization of one's dream. Be positive, therefore, which in no way implies being unrealistic. It in no way means the absence of failure either. Positivity liaises with the overcoming of fear. It moves the individual to face failure as a step and not the end of the road. Thus, in positive attitude, as in action unfettered by fear of failure, President Barrack Obama's submission holds good: "The future rewards those who press on. I don't have time to feel sorry for myself. I don't have time to complain. I'm going to press on." This kind of attitude is no small push forward to truly rewarding passionate action.

When the value of being positive has been sung, it must be acknowledged that ambience significantly sways attitude. Ambience is the setup or environment and the people around us are its most prominent aspect. The people around us therefore have a strong influence on our attitude. This is why it is important to identify and to distinguish between those who mean us well and those who are likely to kill our dreams. Meaning us well does not mean a direct personal engagement with our affairs, though. It may just be their own attitude towards the major things of life that sync or boost rather than quench our dreams. Show me the company you keep and I will tell you who you are, it is proverbially said.

Again, it is not as if with a positive attitude all is on rollercoaster progress. Times and days are bound to come when we experience major downcast; days there will be when we feel inept, unready and unlikely go on; times there will be that, no matter how hard we try, we will feel as if we are in the darkest valley, unable to find any glimpse of direction or energy light. At such times, we must allow the faintest flicker of positive disposition hold us up, allow the dullest glimmer of light to rekindle the faith that there is light at some point not too far off.

It is then clear that, important as goal setting is, great as decision making is, they only get going on the wheel of action. Clear too is it that action itself functions in league with attitude, making a positive mindset a sine qua non of purposeful action because it orders our thought to proactivity.

CHAPTER THREE

ENCOURAGEMENT

The ambience of our operation can be a source of encouragement, including that which can come from within us, from others, from circumstances or from a combination of these. The wisdom or necessity of encouragement is derived from the difficulty of starting off and gunning for a worthwhile goal.

As anyone can testify, starting something new or different can be difficult. At that point, the first problem and enemy of the project can be as close home as our own very self, due to self-inflicted worries about what others would think or say. We are thus self-maimed; we personally tangle up and trip or perhaps just put speed brakes on our own project. Believing in the self becomes mandatory and a major source of encouragement. That belief helps you to get rid of stalling inhibitions.

The topic of encouragement in this discussion requires familiar grounds as reference, which takes us once more to the writing of this book and its halting progress. My encouragement to write came from a lady I encountered, who led me to examine myself for stimulus. That stimulus I found in my own early past, how at the age of twenty-three I had taken a writing course, midway through which I had discontinued. Then some seven years back I decided to write and stopped at the purpose of the book.

She made me glimpse at my own main setbacks; how from within me arose questions and dissuading reasons: "Can I really do this? I have many other things to do and do not have time for writing. Will others find it useful? How useful if useful? Will it be life-transforming enough to warrant my pains?" I was concerned. My husband would say that I was spreading myself thin. These thoughts killed my spirit; they were defeating thoughts. They got me and I convinced myself that this was an impossible task, something to let go, and that I was living in a mere façade. These negative thoughts and impulses multiplied, creating new connections with others and reinforcing existing ones. Predictably, the self-defeating attitude halted the writing project.

When I met the lady I want to refer to as JM, change came dramatically. JM had come for a health visit at the end of which we talked about life in general. She had started and owned five businesses, she said. I was awed by her sheer push.

"Tell me about your businesses," I told JM who took the pains to unravel the complexity of her businesses. My question following her explanation was representative of my awe.

"How many hours do you have in a day?"

"Twenty-four hours, like you," JM replied, with a wink and a smile.

I told her that I was amazed at her ability to convert ideas into practical reality. At the back of my mind lurked the accusation of conscience, a feeling of self-disappointment that I never wrote the book I had tried to write. It was such a preoccupation that it jumped to the fore and I opened it up to her. I had abandoned the project many times, I told her. A lengthy discussion followed.

It was a serendipitous encounter with JM. She asserted that our meeting was no coincidence; that there was a purpose to it. I agreed and interpreted the purpose to be the encouragement I derived from her. I once more decided with this encouraged determination to write the book, which till now had never gone beyond ideas and a few lines. Eventually and finally, I resolved to write.

* * *

Faith in Self: to the heartstring of self-trust every iron string vibrates. Self-trust becomes the magnet, the magnetic field that shapes the alignment of other objects or actions in anyway related to the putative magnet, the self and self-trust. The self turns true to principle characteristic of the magnetic field: describing, defining and influencing objects to take up particular positioning vis-à-vis the magnet, the self.

That evening, I thought of how seven long years had gone by since I thought of the book; how self-created excuses and barriers had held it back; how I had been kept back by negative speculations about its outcome; how it would expose me to criticisms which I couldn't handle. I had to shed my inhibitions. I became convinced that I had something to offer; that I would do my best to not hold back the benefits from the many I envisaged would find value in it.

No sooner had I decided than I went into action. First, I asked my husband to install Microsoft Word to my iPhone. I could write down ideas as they came anytime anywhere—while with my family, faced with a point worth noting, or just when I felt like I had to add a line. It worked; all because I started believing in myself by contagion, as it were, after the encounter with JM. I identified the Word software on my cell phone and consciously decided to create time for writing and then set the time within which to finish the book.

The belief that I could do it started off cycles of inner encouragement and practical implementation. But, not so fast, for another drawback dropped in: I fell sick. That set my agenda back by some three months. Well, I got well and picked up the pieces, not discouraged.

I bring these ups and downs for their lesson: the glow of the finished product hides the rugged path. Proof of this can be observed at just any construction site, any workshop—dust and mud and junk clutter them. When the clean product comes out, we ignore the background, the backdrop. But if we would learn and keep the lesson, the rugged way is the only way, generally speaking. Only fix your eyes upon the goal and your feet upon the path and the goal will come through the misty and rugged drawbacks.

One way to hold on to the path is to define your strengths, which should include the help you can draw on from without. Strengths include experience, survival strategies in previous rough times. They include analytical ability by which to detail out why you feel low, the substance of fear, shame, or criticisms from others. Such feelings could perhaps include the thought of being too late to start, of lagging behind others such as classmates or siblings.

Whatever the case, challenges and difficulties of all types crave encouragement. And this can come in various guises, including strength and courage from the experiences of others. These others may be people you know personally or simply the stories of others you have only heard. You do not have to look far to find help. Someone you know, someone in your family, a school mate or associate who has had a handicap and turned it around into something positive might just be the solution.

Think of that sister, brother, cousin, aunt, or uncle, who has triumphed over difficulties without allowing themselves to be crushed. In the same light, a book you have read or some solution to another challenge might just be the turning point of assistance you need. Think of these and draw inspiration from them, from their situations. You too can triumph over even the worst. You probably know of that friend or co-worker whose house got burnt down and who lost everything but who never gave up. They picked up the pieces and started all over again, perhaps in smaller ways, but contented with that start. Draw strength from these.

It is not necessary to wait for long in the misery of fears. Know diffidence for what it is and get started right away with your dream. Get rid of inner fears, insecurities and do not wallow in discouragement when you encounter a setback in life. Gun for the dream; it is better so. There is nothing in self-pity except lost opportunities and wasted time.

Put positively, what you need to do is believe in and be true to yourself. That faith in your ability to get out of the mess, small as a mustard seed though it be, needs to be stoked. Fan your abilities to flame and raise the banner of hope that no times of challenge will keep you down. Hold it hard that it is a forward march to the achievement point. Faith in yourself is the most solid block in the structural design of your progress, the foundation stone or the 'cornerstone', to use the biblical term. On that solid faith in yourself you can lay one block after another of continued progress. You only need to be persistent and the rest will follow.

Sideline Inhibitors

What others will think and/or say often constitutes a stumbling block to initiative. While sensitivity to the feelings of others is a moral duty, often we allow this to get overblown. Particularly, we do this to add to the convenience and excuse of avoiding the difficulties envisaged in an initiative. We annex the worries of others to augment our own lack of faith in our ability to forge ahead. For the most part, much of what others think of our activities does not mean much. For one thing, except for the few very concerned people in our life, most people do not bother or take serious anything that is not directly relevant to their own wellbeing.

It is unacceptable to let what people think of you hamper or maim you. Really, you are not here to live other people's dreams but yours. Much of what we think is the perception of others is all but our own imagination. We imagine that people are watching our every move and frowning or smiling at us. This is a typical attribute of the impressionable and diffident youth whose conscience is yet undeveloped. Such uncertain youths keep looking out for approval or disapproval from without. They imagine that other people have no other thing in life than to watch, assess and criticize them.

How about circumstances? Sometimes, we have to rely on other things. If a circumstance is hampering you, can you work, can you operate in it? Can you get on under a different circumstance, perhaps not as convenient as the one you envisaged or are used to? The answer to this worry depends on the answer to the question whether there are any alternative ways to get to your goal?

The answer has to be yes; otherwise you are at a dead end. The way with nature and reality is that there are tendencies, directions to effects. You only need the right sensitivity to feel the other possible ways. If one path gets obtruded, take the detour; use the alternative pathway.

Away from nature, alternative means to the same goal are like applying to college/school and having your top five choices. If you are admitted into your first choice, you are happy and go there. However, if you do not get admitted to the school of your first choice, but get into your second choice, then you go there. It used to be a common saying that 'many roads lead to Rome'. The same is true of goals and the means to them.

To pick up the track of my encounter with JM, after the long discussion with her, my perception changed.

"Tell me about your five businesses," I had warmed up to her statement. I lapped up everything she told me about her businesses, especially how she managed her time and coordinated the affairs. That evening and over the next few days, I pondered about the things really holding me back. Most of what I came up with were self-inflicted, self-created. Defeatist thoughts were killing my spirit. I would work the thoughts up to convince myself that the task was impossible and better forgotten about. A physician should have nothing to do with writing, I as good as declared. Alternatively, the drawback was whether, even if I wrote, I would be a good writer. I didn't pause to weigh in on the word good and its various shades. All I needed was a blanket excuse. Like most fears, my excuses flourished in the murk of imprecision, that realm where all color shades blend into one nondescript nebula.

My inhibitions were really blind in that they were not selective enough. They were blinding too as they blocked me from seeing the other side of reality. The talk with JM made me resolve to shed them. But fear generates other fears. I developed a fear of the details. How was it all going to work out? I was not in the right frame of mind to see that once the thought has been judged appropriate and the decision to gun for the goal decided upon, everything would work to the purpose.

Somewhere, I had read of how a drop of water can be as vast as an ocean. It all depended on its proximity. That in the background, I resolved not to be blinded by such an obstacle. That is how I resolved to forge on, to do my best and not to be held back by my own scares.

I had to shed my inhibitions. I resolved to do so. Then another fear (uncertainty) gripped me—the scare about how it would all work out. I felt I would expose myself to criticism and if that happened, what would I do? I worked on my thought process. I knew I had something to offer to many people out there. I kept telling myself that and that I would do my best to not hold back.

Resilience

Given the ruggedness of the normal paths to goals, beyond overcoming personal inhibitions, resilience becomes vital. It is perhaps covered by such terms as perseverance, persistence or patience. Being resilient means matching the ruggedness of the path with personal rebound; it is the refusal to get stuck in the mire, refusal to be worn out by the gruff takes of the way. Given the tough paths, resilience feeds on one solid decision, the decision to not give up anytime, the will to conquer, the unyielding persistence to reach the goal.

There is no guarantee that the plan that you have will go smoothly. In fact, as already insisted upon above, the normal process of any plan is through setbacks. If that is the norm, it stands to reason that you should be armed in advance with an unrelenting, persistent and patient push. Keep your eyes on the ball. Even if the plan suddenly requires a change in tactics, sometimes an almost completely new strategy, keep on. Let the initial dream be lighted in splashing colors. Fan the flames of the fire of your vision with passion by lighting up its final realization and what it will mean to you and to others. Do so and keep going.

Intelligence alone does not achieve. Perseverance in diligent pursuit does and there are examples, especially in academic pursuits that bring this to the limelight. That is why certificates are often resented as the measure of knowledge. For they measure, not knowledge alone, but knowledge plus strategy and persistence. That is why the intelligent person who lacks perseverance would often end up serving the not so intelligent one who does have the patient endurance to drudge through the study program. No goal of value seems to be achievable without perseverance.

Have you ever wondered why brawny and smart people are left on the sidewalks of life, away from the center of social and world changing activities? Consider lack of patient endurance in a specific and challenging field; that is what keeps them at the bottom of the social ladder.

I have had occasion to identify young people who have all it takes in terms of intelligence, brawns and health. Some of them lived from hand to mouth, at the mercy of occasional casual labor. I have volunteered to sponsor several in trades of their choice. To my amazement, I discovered that, despite their talents and in spite of the fact that sponsorship is guaranteed, they often prefer short apprenticeship jobs. One such chose to learn staffing, another tiling, and yet another glasswork! Without exception, these are trades which, although indeed often learned on and polished in the job process, their technical essentials can be acquired within weeks, days or even hours. It is a tendency with those considered less successful—people who do not get to big achievements, despite being highly gifted in many ways. They just pick on the easy-to-achieve things and are contented with them.

Needless to say that the shorter the apprenticeship, the less specialized the trade; that the less specialized a trade, the less likely it is to put its owner at the center of great things. If you want to build tall, plant your foundations deep. The eucalyptus tree, known to reach

90 meters, also grows deep taproot that reaches some 12-meter depths within two years. Besides, its roots spread far out, beyond the width of its canopy. Such lessons from nature we must learn: to reach high, go deep.

There is no demeaning of any job or work in this perspective. Every service, even the less acclaimed, has its own value. Nonetheless, if you think of specializing in the less specialized job, so to speak; if you want to make a common utility your focus, do be fully engaged in it; do make a mark in it by being something of an expert. In other words, be meticulous and devote quality time in training and execution so as to do the so-called simple things with refinement. Do not settle for the easy-to-do, but make what is apparently easy-to-do so refined that it is obvious that you are out for the best in your field of specialization. In other words, add depth to what otherwise looks one-dimensional or trite.

Depth requires patience, stubborn patience, patience that matches the challenging tasks in the process of goal achievement. Each goal for each person will present different challenges, some hard, others mild. While some goals will be reached with little to talk about in terms of challenges, most goals of worth are through rugged routes. A combination of the tough as of the mild challenges calls for resilient persistence and patience.

To be sure, there are plains and plateaus to traverse for some, which does not mean that the way is obstruction free or not undulating or curving round and chuting through thickets and thorns, though. However, for others, besides the ruggedness of the path, there is the incline with varying steepness, sometimes with ledges that provide dangling, hair's breadth daring chances of reaching over, besides being slippery. For some, it is mountains to climb and every mountain, for the most part, presents challenges similar to those posed by the hill. However, for the mountain, an additional difficulty is of longer duration, requiring greater stamina. If the goal is worth it, if you matched your chances at the start and strategized before making your decision, then keep it up; use a detour if necessary; retract and reroute if required; keep the beat and steam to reach the coveted goal; be resilient.

When we cross over from decision and action to the need for encouragement, therefore, shades of this encouragement come into play. You need to trust the iron string of your own person and endowments, tap on side help while staying clear of side inhibitors as well as being resilient. That is to say that encouragement finally thrives on personal rebound, even if support comes from various other sources.

CHAPTER FOUR

THE TEAM

In the pursuit of the goal, there is no way you can ignore the involvement of others. So, it is not just the *what* but the *who* as well. Who gets to be involved with me in the process, the team to carry through to the goal? Clearly, the know-all and do-it-all-by-myself one-man-up days are gone. Cooperation has come to stay as the new order, individuals only chipping in their quota of expertise in the complex of general achievement. This, no doubt is a situation-imposed humility; but humility it is; and humility is demanded, however it is qualified.

The tricky twitch here is that, while you do not necessarily spin or squirm at the beck and call of other people's opinion, while you do not turn at their command or play by their whims, you do need to concert with them. The world has shades of nuances and each person has blind spots. Luckily, we all have blind spots at different points. Luckily, others can see better where their fellow blind-spotted actors do not. Luckily, reason informs us that needing help from another person is but natural. Therefore, without hesitation, ask for needed help. It does not belittle you.

Not only should you seek help for particular issues, you need a support network of persons who can uphold your cause and cheer you on. Friends? Yes; more than friends—a team. A team is the strength of the vulnerable. All the team needs is dependability, loyalty, trustworthiness of each member. This will ensure that team members do not take advantage of the vulnerability of each other. Team members tap on the strength of each other. They buoy each other up.

Team members are sourced from diverse competencies and may be drawn from among family relations and friends. Colleagues and experts too are handy. Each will supply particular assistance at a given juncture. As a team, all constitute a solid base from which to rise to great achievement.

The help that other people offer is not always sustaining, however. Sometimes, for various individual reasons, putdown attitudes from those who are expected to help you will be directed at your person. The point might be to break your spirit or to satisfy their own ego cravings and designs. The catch is that such attitudes may read to you like expert ratings. They might make you feel worthless or incapable of any worthwhile achievement. You feel as if you failed an objective test or examination conducted with appropriate impartiality. Really, can that be the case? On what bases do such approaches gain the favor to be so valuably neutral? Do not buy it; do not let them build up a negative self-image in you. Hold it as a basic database on yourself that at the very worst, you are worth far more and better than any expert can decide. You are a complex, with inexhaustible possibilities and endowments.

Come to think of it, while criticisms may be corrective, an attitude of know-it-all, even from an expert, is false. The bad thing is that, in spite of its groundlessness, it can and is often destructive to the personality of another person. What you need to know is that opinions are only opinions until you personalize and adopt them. Also know that the person criticizing you might just be using you as an excuse for their own devious purposes. And when you critically consider the moral right of the critique, you just might find them too as blameworthy or very near the things for which they blame and put you down. Experts and critics are as much liable to failures as anyone else. One unwarranted and hence point of failure or dispute is their assessment of you. Is it possible that they are rather projecting their own weaknesses and doing so with vengeance? You should be able to measure the extent to which they can rightly and genuinely point out your inexactitudes or failings.

Success is in the marketplace of life and available for all, not just for others. You are wired with and for success. So, success is meant for you, no less than for others. People have different talents and you just might be receiving putdowns from those who think that only their own way or talents should be considered. That should not be. The world is a vast playing ground, offering each individual room to exercise different skills. It is not because someone has more experience than you at a given point that they should rate you destructively. Given time, effort and focus, not even the sky should limit you. The human being, they say, is the most versatile and adaptable creature on earth and that is the race to which you belong. There is hardly any field of service any of us would not adapt to and even reach some level of expertise, given the right nurturing.

At all cost, then, dump the feeling of ineptitude and of worthlessness. Those are negative emotions that bring no one any good; they are vexatious and massively progress-defeating. So, it is best to not only avoid occasions that generate such feelings, but to avoid such people as well. The well-known *desiderata* tells us to "avoid loud and aggressive people; they are vexation to the spirit". Avoid people and occasions that make you feel unworthy in a destructive way. Any occasion or person that does not offer constructive criticism, but rather makes you feel you are not good enough or cannot be as good as them is anathema. Avoid them like the plague.

Directly, negative persons and occasions apart, there are the overwhelming, personality-imposing type of persons who sweep you off your feet and out of your fief. Your personality becomes a mere shadow of their own. Such people want you to go where they choose or design. They want you to do what *they* want. For that reason, they impose their wants and perspectives on you. In consequence, overwhelmed, you start reading your own perspectives and dreams as worthless.

Familiar ground, innate talents are where your strength resides. Military battles are often won by the principle of familiarity with one key item or the other. Even intelligence really often reads as simple familiarity with the subject matter. Familiarity with something as direct as knowledge of the terrain or ambience is already an advantage. Now, your own familiar terrain is your strong point as expressed in your dreams and planned means of achieving them. Failure often follows the attempt to live somebody else's dream. That is why, for all their good intentions, some parents have frustrated their children by imposing parental dreams on them. You can be ruined by pursuing the dreams of others. You can be ruined by using other people's methods instead of your own that is bound up with your dreams and your innate or spontaneous approaches to them. And even in the animal kingdom, the principle of familiarity with one's terrain can mean life or death for one animal or the other. It is wisdom that has been tapped by humanity as ancient as research can reach back in time.

In vain would an animal as ravaging and fearless as a lion pursue the rabbit which keeps to the proximity of its abode. The caveman was able to tap on this wisdom against the marauding savagery of really powerful preying animals. Adventurously, the caveman mastered the limited space of the cave. The troglodyte could hide behind a boulder, perch on a high point, get to the inner chambers or descend to caverns within the caves unknown to the invader. Simple: familiarity was such an advantage.

By the same token, preying animals tend to pull their quarry to their own familiar grounds. That is how the crocodile can outmaneuver the tiger, leopard or lion by pulling them to its own field. The lion in its lair indicates absolute advantages. It has even been detailed that Nathaniel (in the bible) sitting under the fig tree (as Jesus indicates to him) illustrates the homeliness of a man at ease in his own environment, his familiar grounds. A man with the fig tree for shade is a man in his familiar sphere, a thing which betokens confidence born of knowledge of his environment. It is such a one that the judge of the universe declares to be "without a trace of guile". Such a one is authentic and exudes integrity in gait and intentions.

Cistercian and Benedictine monks often evoke the value of familiar ground by saying that a monk out of his community is like fish out of water. Sure ground is often safe ground, and by 'sure' here is meant familiar ground. In saying this, I am aware of the possibility of exceptions and of the verity that all comparisons are lame, imperfect and incomplete. Yet, it is firmly established that outside of one's fief, away from your sphere of home advantage, is perilous grounds.

The purpose of this emphasis is to drive home the lesson: Don't let others pull you to compete with them in their own field and sphere of excellence. Pull back and away to your turf. It is in the strange setting that you are likely to be brought down, preyed upon and proved inefficient by others. It is in the unfamiliar ground, the alienating setting that you are likely to be made to feel perennially one step below others. Resist it.

Avoid people who crush your every idea. They might just well be working out their envy of your phenomenal relevance and progress. Their worry (perhaps unconsciously harbored) might be that you would excel and beat them at it. So, they pull you to grounds familiar to themselves but unfamiliar to you. There, they make you know that you are lost, as indeed you are in the new place where they then brand you as nobody. There they want to make you believe that they are always right, that they always have the better idea or opinion than yours; that you always have to learn from them and they have nothing to learn from you. Step back and see how this is against commonsense.

The principle of familiarity with one's environment or subject matter is illustrated in the story of a reputably brilliant English and Literature educator in Cameroon. One early morning, the said literary guru had driven forty-five minutes from Bamenda to Ndop where he lectured. Upon reaching the entrance to the town, something rattled inside the bonnet and the car ceased. As providence would have it, a youth of about fourteen years, looking ragged and dull was passing by. The greased and oil-stained attire of the youth suggested to the lecturer that he could be a mechanic in training. So he beckoned the young man and explained his plight to him. Silently, with a dull and inexpressive face, the young man opened the bonnet and in about three minutes had identified the fault and resolved it.

That, to the lecturer, illustrated the principle of familiarity with subject matter as intelligence. If by the youth's outward look and uncouth comportment the lecturer judged him primitive and unintelligent, the young man was actually well-informed about his trade technicalities; he was tidy in his knowledge of the car engine. Proof was in the pointed, rather clinical manner in which the youth approached the car malfunction. The friend lecturer said that there was no doubt that he too would have discovered the problem eventually, albeit slowly, given that the problem was observably mechanical. However, he adds, that would have costed him far more time in groping search for the clue. He would, besides, have dirtied himself with his clumsy groping in the process. In addition, his limited knowledge would have kept him in a mental state of panic at the possibility of a relapse of the malfunction. He lacked the intelligence and advantage of familiarity with the subject matter, was his conclusion.

Those who spend their time judging others (except themselves), considering themselves perfect as against everyone else's *glaring* imperfections; those who think that they are to dictate the life pattern of everyone—avoid them. They manifest what in other discussions would be termed pride and presumptiveness. In the context of this discussion, they are compassionately not judged but simply seen as pulling others to their own familiar ground, trying to get to a vantage point over them. You could say that they are full of themselves and managing to crush others' confidence, thus indirectly taking control of them. Their tactical or rather Machiavellian technique is to draw people out of themselves. They work it out to take others away from their talents and comfort zones where they are likely to fare best.

Do not be so waylaid, entrapped and made use of; do not be sold so cheaply into projecting yourself or allowing yourself to be projected as useless. At the risk of saying it ad nauseam, remember that no human owns you; that you are your own person, with your own unique gifts and talents God-given. So, your reality should not be determined by others. Do not leave it to them to manipulate you and to pose to develop your dream for you. The dream is yours, yours from God as enunciated in this beautiful poetic piece attributed to Charles Peguy (1873-1914), French poet, essayist and editor:

The Heart of the Matter

God said: I myself will dream a dream within you...
Good dreams come from me, you know...
My dreams seem impossible,
not too practical,
not for the cautious man or woman...
a little risky sometimes
a trifle brash perhaps...

Some of my friends prefer
to rest more comfortably
in sounder sleep,
with visionless eyes…

But for those who share my dreams
I ask a little patience,
a little humor,
some small courage,
and a listening heart,
I will do the rest.

Then they will risk and wonder at their daring…
Run, and marvel at their speed…
Build, and stand in awe at the beauty of their building.

You will meet me often at your work…
In your companions, who share the risk
In your friends, who believe in you enough
to lend you their own dreams,
their own hands,
their own hearts,
to your building;
in the people who stand in your doorway,
stay a while
and walk away, knowing that they too
can find a dream.

There will be sun-filled days

and sometimes it will rain—
a little variety.
Both come from me.
So, come now; be content—
It is my dream you dream,
my house you build,
my caring you witness,
my love you share.
And this is the heart of the matter.

* * *

If by the above discussion on negativity brought on by negative/destructive criticism the impression is that all criticism must be denounced, then there is a misinterpretation of the point. There is healthy, image-building and prospects-building criticism. You know healthy criticism from many fronts. Primarily, it is couched in politeness. The positive values of the criticized are pointed out and then the negative point brought in as (perhaps a sizable) blot on the good. The drift in healthy criticism is that the criticized person's dream is seen in the light of fitting their abilities and inclinations. The critic thus comes out as enabling you to reach those goals by suggesting ways to better your progress. The critic offers bolsters along with the strong impression that you already are quite impressive with your dream processes.

As a matter of fact, positive criticism does not break; it molds and propagates. A closer look at it reveals it more as counsel than criticism. It is a critique that is accompanied by suggestions. It is not the acrid putdown that breaks down rather than builds. It is prophetically said of Jesus in Isaiah 42:2-3 that, besides not crying or shouting out aloud, "He does not break the crushed reed or snuff the faltering wick..." We could expound the crying and shouting to mean abrasiveness or even tantrums and hysteria over what is noticed as improper in another person's general process of achievement. The smoldering fire, in this case, would stand for the flagging point in goal setting and pursuit. This is it; proper criticism buoys up; it does not sink the storm-tossed vessel.

This propriety in criticism can be sourced in the positioning of the critic. If from without, lacking intimacy with the facts and person being criticized, the likelihood is that the critic's rating would be superficial, and untrue. By intimacy with the realities and the personality involved with them, the critic approaches the subject and matter from an insider position and an empathetic poise. If, even with such intimacy, the critic fails to point out the good and beautiful aspects before referring to the blot on it, it would be obvious that the critic's purpose is not genuine, not meant to correct but rather to destroy. In that light, the critic is unwelcome, their criticism being anathema to the would-be goal achiever.

In no way is this to be considered an invitation to bitterness for being criticized, however. You do not need to engage in blame game, either; bitterness only holds you back, works against you, eats you up. When you are bitter, you blur your prospects and vision. You scramble up your dream, thus restraining your creative ingenuity, your innate creativity. With bitterness, you get blinded to the open doors; you miss the open doors of breakthroughs. Opportunities might well not exist if the person for whom they are provided is blind to them. If focus shifts from the goal, vision, or dream to the object of bitterness, you are obviously left with just bitterness as your goal. You cannot plant bitterness and expect to harvest sweetness from it. In bitterness, negative thoughts luxuriate. It should be stated that negative thoughts are to bitterness what flies are to exposed and rotting meat: they (the flies of bitterness) swarm in and continue in noisy nuisance.

How do you get off the bitter leech? You cannot just think bitterness away. To empty air from a container, fill it with gasoline or some other liquid. To drive out darkness, switch on the light. Just as nothing comes of nothing, nothing goes away for nothing either. To get rid of bitterness, therefore, cultivate sweetness. Positively, go after gentle ways, polite ways, and constructive methods. In other words, gun for what you *want to do* not what you *want to avoid*. You cannot run away from evil and you cannot fight it by wishing it away. The way out is substitution: replace bitterness with goodness in concrete terms. Return to your dreams and pursue them with vigor; defy the challenges.

Challenges thrust themselves on us from various causes—a poorly conceived decision we make, a mistake of ours or of another person. Sometimes it is hard to pin the source of problems because they are so entangled in the normal flow of reality that piecing it up is really hard. Life may dish out to us illnesses, whether contracted or congenital; life may thrust upon us the unaccountable death of a loved one or saddle us with a calamity, such as our house going up in flames; life may expose us to the unexpected harassment of wicked people, leading to physical or psychological bruises, deep wounds of abuse, rape or other forms of odious cruelty.

Problems brought about by our mistakes can engender a feeling of guilt. Guilt itself becomes a problem on its own. In the event, self-forgiveness becomes a first and often very hard step. For one of the hardest things to do, whether of self or others, is forgiveness.

Forgiveness needs to be looked at in the right perspective. First and philosophically speaking, we need to bear in mind that perfection is not of this world. It takes little effort for anyone to realize that there is nothing without blemish. Blemish is always noticed somehow, whether in tone, complexion, applicability or worth. To be perfect, a thing needs be, not only exact in proportion and strength; not only value-exact, but also somewhat valid for use in all times and places. Otherwise, there will be a time or place where such a thing does not fit and is therefore not of perfect value and validity. Actually, to be perfect, an object needs to be God. Now, none of us, our neighbor or co-worker is God. Simply put, imperfections are only in the nature of things.

When mistakes lead to devastating consequences, however, there is no way to pretend that they do not matter. When mistakes are repeated also, it is clear that carelessness or nonchalance is at play, that greater effort at stemming them is required. So, both effort and acceptance are needed in the face of ours and others' mistakes. We must consider letting go as a basic issue in the process of forgiveness. Forgiveness itself is knotty, requiring all the help we can muster, which is why divine grace through prayer is considered one of the handiest means. Prayer, inter alia, is proclaimed intention and desire to the ultimate mover of all things. Sometimes this is done through various intermediaries, such as angelic spirits and saintly ancestors.

You might hear hurt people say: "I can't just pretend that this never happened; I can't just pretend that he/she never did this to me." They are right. No one is asking anyone to pretend. In fact, the proportion and intensity of the harm done to us or by us needs to be *properly envisaged* and *declared* in the first place. To forgive, it has been said, basically means to let go. Now, this *letting* go cannot be of nothing but of something. The harm or consequences of any given mistake needs to be clearly enunciated before being forgiven. Forgiveness is not about covering up. It is about proper exposure, acknowledgement and a constructive path to ensure that it does not get repeated. It is a letting go in the spirit of permanence and genuine efforts to preclude both further errors and their consequences.

Like proper criticism, forgiveness is a wonderfully positive thing with magnificent healing outcomes. It is a wise turn. No wonder, Jesus expounded on its necessity in outlandishly challenging images – turning the other cheek, going two miles when asked to go one…Yet, once committed, mistakes are permanent part of our past. They are part of the whole. Yet we must guard against piling them up to have the greater ratio. Piling mistakes upon mistakes mars by making us perennially mistake makers. You become what you repeat or stay long in company of. An idler is one who spends more time in leisure and less time at work. A thief is not a man who once stole, but one who habitually steals. To become something, do it often or be more often in its company. And so, letting go of mistakes lets us into a new path, into light and into life. It is pitched on the resolve and strategies to forestall any recurrence.

The casual phrase often heard—forgive and forget—must be appreciated for its rhythmic, alliterative and assonantal effects, but perhaps not for its verity. Forgiving someone is a clearly voluntary choice but forgetting is not quite so voluntary. The wisdom of errors is that we remember them and their impact so as to avoid repeating them or similar errors. While deliberately visualizing and dwelling on mistakes must be dissuaded, any effort at forgetting soon turns out to reinforce what they are out to stop. However, forgetting mistakes has everything to do with acting as if bygones *are* really bygones—gone by, remembered no more than a fully healed wound, even if it leaves traces on the skin. Forgetting, therefore, is figurative and means highlighting the lesson learned rather than wiping the memory of the mistake. It has everything to do with understanding that the offender and the offence are not of choice permanence, but a side-track from which to walk away. Yet, the lesson and how it makes you a better person, with wiser steps to better choices, must be cultivated.

It can be said that while remembering the past may be important and even healthy, dwelling on the lurid or gory elements of that past is not. For we become what we tarry with, in a sense. The gory or painful part of the past, its details, would tend to replicate the negative and depressive emotions. And, as already pointed out, these are things to be replaced with the positive and uplifting emotions.

We become what we think, and what we think, we become. In other words, you can tell the health of the tree from its fruit or expect the kind of fruit from the health of the tree. So much so is this that even Jesus gets surprised that the leafy fig tree has no fruit. He shows his indignation by cursing it to wither. If by error or choice we dwell on the gruesome, that would spike gloomy and gruesome emotions which we are likely to put to use directly or indirectly. Negative feelings have a consistency in being costly. A jocular anecdote on the cost of hatred, which can be replicated with regard to other negative sentiments, runs roughly as follows:

Being a passionate businessman open to buy and sell all I can, I set out to investigate the cost of a cup of hatred. That is how I came to present my need to the salesman who, taking a deep breath, started listing the stakes to me:

Shattered peace, incurable worries that will eat up your heart up and spew out deep bitterness at sight of the hated object; when others try to celebrate him or her, you will be cramped in a prowling posture intent on contradicting them and proving that the hated person does not deserve the feast. At sight of the person, you will lose all joy and when he or she laughs, tears will roll down your cheeks. While others project great things, you will busy yourself seeking hooks and ropes to pull your hated quarry down. The spirit of God will leave you to the wiles of the devil and the play place of demons.

Health issues will plague you, including high blood pressure, with diabetes and perhaps stroke or even cancer, liver and kidney diseases as you drink from the cup of hate, bitterness, grudge, unforgiveness, malice, anger, jealousy, envy, and resentment. Neither prayers nor drugs will serve any purpose and you are sure to die before your time and chute straight for hell...

While the seller was still detailing the cost of hatred, the businessman sneaked off, devastated by the colossal cost of the business item he sought. He was convinced that hatred came from gossip that painted negative pictures of others and that once the negative picture takes root in the individual, hatred is sparked.

* * *

A thirty-five-year-old single mother whom I will here call Christie spent years taking care of her mother who was suffering from Alzheimer's disease. It was challenging for Christie who also had a full-time job. Eventually, her mother passed on and Christie and her dad needed to prepare for the funeral. That is how, in the course of sorting out her mother's things, Christie and her dad came upon some old notes and letters of her mom. Among these was a letter which her mom had written many years back, before the Alzheimer's disease took hold of her. In the letter, she specified that Christie was not her husband's child.

You can imagine how devastating this was for Christie. So, the man that Christie had always believed to be her dad was not her biological father. Christie's dad was more than shocked to learn that the child he had always believed was his own was not his biological daughter. He too was baffled. As Christie narrated this, I asked her how she felt.

"Very hurt, disappointed, angry," she said.

Her dad felt betrayed, very angry and hurt.

Well, Christie decided to carry on and to give her mother a befitting funeral.

"I am trying to find a place in my heart to forgive her. My dad is very angry. I have told him that mom is dead. 'You have to forgive her. You have to let go,'" she said.

Sometimes, forgiveness is in the process of positive action towards the wrongdoer. We perhaps need to recall the discussed idea of substitution: we put in good deeds to displace the evil of unforgiveness.

* * *

While we are on the topic of the influence of others, it should be emphasized that motives for goals should be innate and not from competitiveness. What is born of external influence ends up being unsatisfactory, even if success seems to have been achieved. The truth is that such externalized goals do not take root in the reality of our inner selves. That is why even at the peak of apparent success, emptiness and a lack of fulfillment is experienced. The so-called success in that case is very ephemeral. It is external, unfounded and unable to stand a reality check.

While pushfulness and self-assertion are virtues to be cultivated or encouraged as a means to higher goals, unhealthy competition with others is in bad taste. Rather, each person should pick out the best to imitate in others and compete with the self. An African adage has it that no two fingers are the same. And the popular *desiderata* has it that "If you compare yourself with others, there will always be better and lesser people than you are…" This argues for you to be your own yardstick. Let time be your ever toughening measurement. By it, where you check on where you were before and where you should be now. Do of course congratulate and celebrate every stride you make, and reward them or yourself, as the case may be.

CHAPTER FIVE

PRAYER

Casually mentioned earlier was prayer as an aid in the pursuit of goals and in the process of forgiveness. I cannot over-emphasize the importance of prayer, given my personal experience of its phenomenal power and effects. Prayer has done phenomenal things in my life. Jottings on the effects are more than a book can hold.

Since I am recommending what works, I can freely propose that you, the reader of these pages should make God part of your life project, overseer of everything you do, every decision you make. He is not only the God of all consolation, but he is the God of hope. From Him you can obtain an end to pessimism and fearfulness of sad events and tragedies. You can obtain divine counsel from the Holy Spirit and be shown the way to go about everything.

It would be sad if you do not believe in God and his providential power, a thing taken for granted in this book, even though religion is not really our project herein. Nonetheless, the tilt here is towards those who are already believers but who, as often happens, might state that they do not know how to pray. And that is the challenge when they narrow prayer to protestations in pious-sounding banalities. For to some, prayer is about using big words or providing grandiose titles for God. Verbal colorfulness is only helpful in prayer if it enhances concentration. A few words about prayer might disillusion anyone holding such views.

In prayer, you relate or communicate with the divine transcendent being, the Heavenly Father. There is nothing grandiloquent about communicating genuinely with a loving personality. Truth to self, authenticity in the enunciation of our needs or in praise is simply what it is all about. The underlying concept here is how honesty finds the heart of the Lord. We do not need to put up a show for God to hear and answer us. In simplicity and authentic expression of the self we can experience God's presence, his touch of love and power.

Prayer can take several forms – talking, singing, reciting, meditating, silence and listening. What is important is the communication element, whether verbal or otherwise; commune with your Heavenly Father as it befits you. This might mean employing one or several forms at once or alternating the forms.

Somehow, *speaking* out our mind to God has come to be the expected form of prayer; yet the other forms of prayer are just as valid and it can be said without fear of contradiction that the essential thing in the prayer process is to put ourselves in the divine presence by our intentions. The rest follows hitch free.

Without sounding like a book of prayer, a brief look at the listed forms of prayer would be in order here.

Often, the assumed norm of prayer is talking, talking about the things uppermost in our mind and life to God—our life goals, our career, our parents, siblings, health and needs. We request God to see to our wellbeing and to forestall all dangers and lack. We ask Him to ensure that goodness follows us all the days of our life. The range of needs in this respect is unlimited and there are people who detail the conditions and ambience of their needs to such an extent that it sounds as if they are giving God a serious lecture on realities surrounding. God should hear from them!

A thing to remember in oral/prayer talk is that our enunciated circumstances are only a way of invoking God's presence or reminding ourselves of His omnipresence. So doing, we take shelter in it, assuring ourselves that in the shadow of his wings all our needs would be met. The words are only reassurances to ourselves that bring us into His presence.

Alternative to talking is singing or reciting. Again, these have the same purpose—ensconcing ourselves in the reassuring presence of God. The prayer part is surrendering ourselves to his will as in the prayer of Charles de Focauld:

> *Father, I abandon myself into your hands; do with me what you will. Into your hands I commend my spirit; I offer it to you with all the love of my heart for I love you, Lord, and so need to give myself, to surrender myself into your hands without reserve and with boundless confidence, for you are my Father.*

Yes, indeed, for before we were formed in our mother's womb, God knew and knows us through and through, as the psalmist says. This thrusts into the practice of singing or recitations of psalms, holy songs, written words that capture our inner sentiments, set prayers, or the rosary.

I have found psalms 34 and 118 very uplifting when all seems lost for me. Other psalms, writings or songs can capture our sentiments and uplift us. John Foley S.J.'s song, "The Lord Hears the Cry of the Poor" roves among and merges several verses of Psalm 34 (verses 2-3, 6-7, 18-19, 23) — a merger of praise, consolation, comfort, assurance, and the assertion that God is our refuge. The intensity somewhat depletes when the words are not accompanied by the melody, but the essence can be sensed:

The Cry of the Poor

The Lord hears the cry of the poor.
Blessed be the Lord.

I will bless the Lord at all times,
with praise ever in my mouth.
Let my soul glory in the Lord,
who will hear the cry of the poor.

The Lord hears the cry of the poor.
Blessed be the Lord.

Let the lowly hear and be glad:
the Lord listens to their pleas;
and to hearts broken God is near,
who will hear the cry of the poor.

The Lord hears the cry of the poor.
Blessed be the Lord.

Every spirit crushed God will save;
will be ransom for their lives;
will be safe shelter for their fears,
and will hear the cry of the poor.

The Lord hears the cry of the poor.
Blessed be the Lord.
We proclaim your greatness, O God,
your praise ever in our mouth;
every face brightened in your light,
for you hear the cry of the poor.

So comforting has Foley's song been to me, such a reassurance that God is with me, particularly at the time I was going through some difficulties. I have referred others going through difficult times to it and the feedback from these people indicates that they too have reaped of its consolation.

Of the same soothing experience has been 'On Eagle's wings', a rendition of Psalm 91 by Father Jan Michael Joncas:

You who dwell in the shelter of the Lord,
who abide in his shadow for life,
say to the Lord: "My refuge, my rock in whom I trust!"

And he will raise you up on eagle's wings,
bear you on the breath of dawn,
make you to shine like the sun,
and hold you in the palm of his hand.

The snare of the fowler will never capture you,
and famine will bring you no fear:
under his wings your refuge,
his faithfulness your shield.

And he will raise you up on eagle's wings,
bear you on the breath of dawn,
make you to shine like the sun,
and hold you in the palm of his hand.

You need not fear the terror of the night,

nor the arrow that flies by day;
though thousands fall about you,
near you it shall not come.

And he will raise you up on eagle's wings,
bear you on the breath of dawn,
make you to shine like the sun,
and hold you in the palm of his hand.

For to his angels he's given a command
to guard you in all of your ways;
upon their hands they will bear you up,
lest you dash your foot against a stone.

And he will raise you up on eagle's wings,
bear you on the breath of dawn,
make you to shine like the sun,
and hold you in the palm of his hand.

I held close to this reassuring song when I suffered the loss of my aunt and my mother (see chapter 6), the song bearing me through life's burning/purifying flames. To this day, I often use it in prayer, but it came in most valuably handy when I fell on painful times.

Sometimes, especially when one is going through a tough time, praying becomes a challenge, a painful experience which I have had several times. It is quite a common experience as testified by many of the people with whom I have talked on the issue. So, you are not alone if you fall into such moments. If you find it difficult to pray when depressed, discouraged, down and out; if you find yourself unable to pray with many words, or find that your prayer is only somewhat of lip mouthing without any feeling of pious reassurance, know that it is normal and so do not give up. Perhaps you do not need so many words; use fewer words, words that perhaps best capture your predicament. It is okay to just say 'Jesus, I trust in you". And remember that, as we said before, the essence of prayer is being in the presence of God. A gentle reminder by evocation, using a few words, is enough.

Supposing you have such a difficult day ahead that you feel overwhelmed and restless; naturally, you are unable to get into any contemplative prayer. Suffice it for you to say, 'Lord, give me the strength to go through today'. It is not by loud cries, gesticulations or elaborate pietistic talk that our prayer is gaged. Your Father in Heaven hears your every word and knows you through and through. He knows what you are going through, a truth captured in the anonymous song heard in some African churches: "He knows it all":

He knows my thoughts, my ways, my deeds; my Jesus knows it all
E'ry part in me His hands hath made; He knows, He knows it all
He knows (He knows) it all, my total heart (He knows).
Nothing is hidden from my Lord; He knows, He knows

it all.

In the darkness or bright sunlight, He knows, He knows it all.
In depths beneath or heights above, (He knows) He knows it all.
What e'er I do (I do), what e'er I say (He knows),
He notes and takes into account what e'er I do or say.

He plans my way; He directs me; He knows, He knows it all.
In time of woe, in time of joy, He's there and knows it all.
His plan for me (for me), is in His hands (He knows).
He plans and controls everything, yes! Jesus knows it all.

My life on earth, my Jesus knows, His hands provide me strength.
If I should leave this earthly home, Jesus has one for me.
Jesus loves me (loves me), beyond compare (compare).
I am the sheep of His pasture; He loves me, this I know.

My life's mysteries my Jesus knows, He knows and cares for me.
No matter how the tides may rise, He's there and will take care.
My times (my times) are ever in His hands (His hands);

He draws the plan and executes as it is in His hand.

* * *

It is in place here to mention the rosary and the mysteries they celebrate. The rosary comes under various forms of prayer—recitation, invocation and meditation, for sure. But differentiating kinds of prayer can be misleading. For at the end of the day, prayer, as already said, is communion with God, being in His presence, accepting his decision by aligning our desires with His will. So then, the rosary as meditation is drawing out sentiments that keep us glued to one or the other aspect or reality of God.

Believing in the living word of God, whether read or proclaimed by us or others to us, is a way of logging unto what God says or what is said of Him in scripture as in other forms of inspired words, songs or recitations. The rosary, which draws almost entirely on scripture, provides a landing or kick off pad, an altar or pulpit from which the praying person makes petitions.

Details apart, the joyful, luminous, sorrowful and glorious mysteries celebrate the life of Christ and his mother, all outlined in scriptures. Reciting the Ave Maria and other prayers sequenced in the rosary keeps us attuned to God's interventions in human history, thus drawing His presence to our notice. We shelter in that protective presence and make specific requests for His interventions. Said in sincerity and earnestness, our prayers are preconditioned by their alignment to God's will. If we have absorbed His closeness and His nature as we recount the mysteries, then we synchronize with His will and receive what we ask for.

* * *

Let me hasten here to say that prayer is a proactive assertion and acceptance of God's will. In prayer we enunciate our desires and needs, but submit them to the modifications necessitated by His infinite wisdom, which is for our own and the greater good of all the world.

My pet phrase about prayer is: do everything to be in God's presence and then do what you want. This inspiration is drawn from Genesis 17:1, "Walk before me and be perfect", a commission given by God to Abraham "our father in faith". It is no doubt a concept difficult to appreciate— that the essence of prayer is not requests to be granted, but synchronicity with God's will; not miracles to be witnessed, but yielding and self-surrender. Yet, it is in the spirit of the just quoted scripture that walking in God's presence and being blameless is rewarded with plenty: "And I will make my covenant between me and you, and will multiply you exceedingly." While the literal sense is that Abraham's progeny shall be plentiful, it is not amiss to also take it to mean that his needs shall be met with abundance. In this respect, prayers answered often simply means that the praying person notices that what was prayed for has somehow been provided. If it comes in the exact package requested, then it is considered as a miracle.

When we align ourselves with God's will and are in his presence, our every desire, wish or need becomes a petition to Him. This is the wisdom both of silence as prayer and of contemplative prayer. A beautiful line of Rabbi Jonathan Sacks reads, "Create moments of silence in your soul if you want to hear the voice of God." Everything falls into place when we get lost in the folds of divine love and will by silence. The difference between invocation or the popular forms of prayer and absolute silence is that in the former we turn our attention to notice and commune with the divine presence. In silence, we are aware, without necessarily voicing any specific need to the divine presence. It is enough that we are soaked in that presence— "calmed and quieted…like a child quieted at its mother's breast" (Ps. 131:2)

Yet, even silent prayer is also an active thing as opposed to the passivism or the quietism of seventeenth century France, Italy and Spain associated with the heretical writings of Father Miguel de Molinos, and later of the likes of François Malaval and Madame Guyon. We go into silence "seeking the face of God", not blankness. There is no arguing the fact that there is a sense in which blankness means blighting out things created in order to log in on the Ground of our being, the ultimate reality, God. But that is a rarified perception subject to a lot of misunderstanding and abuse. It is best avoided. For it is easy to misinterpret this objective emptiness; it is safer to enunciate and pursue the more understandable form—the *person* rather than the thing or emptiness of God.

When the road seems dark then, when you are weary, confused or agitated, remember II Corinthians 9:12—"My grace is enough for you" and keep up the efforts. Keep setting your goals and keep being focused in the right direction. Your Heavenly Father will do the rest. You only need to trust Him; do learn to trust.

So, sometimes, you do not have to say anything at all other than place yourself in God's presence. Silence is thus a form of prayer, not least because in it God whispers to us. The world being generally too noisy, silence is a way to God who underlies all its reality, all the bustle and vitality of the world which, because of the noise, we fail to notice or hear Him in. But, whether we make petitions, invocations, meditate or contemplate, silence should be a central component of the prayer routine.

The all-important task of living in the presence of God can be helped by chaining, what Tennyson in the poem "Morte d'Arthur" pictorially describes as "bound by gold chains about the feet of God" after remarking that "more things are wrought by prayer than this world dreams of." So, apart from praying earnestly, ask others to chain up and to pray for you and your intentions. When and with whom you feel comfortable to share specific intentions, do so. But when you do not feel like sharing such intimacies, simply ask others to pray for your intentions.

Let it also be remembered that action reinforces prayer and vice versa. So, when you pray, it is no virtue to fold your arms and sit waiting for things to miraculously happen. Grace builds on nature and we have to be participants in the sovereign will of God. We are not to wait for that will to be forced on us. An African proverb says, "While waiting, be on the way, moving." For, although miracles do occur, for the most part, prayers are answered with opportunities for us to take advantage of. Such opportunities include people coming your way to give us direct help or provide the emotional and psychological strength to carry on, making (in different ways) a difficult road easier.

Therefore, while you pray, be engaged in vigorous efforts at resolving your situation. Let answered prayer find you ready, awake and with trimmed, oil-filled lamps. Ask, yes, but also seek a headway. Knock at doors of opportunities. Nurse the belief in your ability to tilde over as you pray. Prove your faith by anticipatory action. Be proactive in relation to prayer and the things asked for. That is how belief and action will enhance your faith, which itself is able to surmount the mountains of doubt.

We find prayer and answered prayer to be composite, a blended unit of human and divine will. It is a cooperation of the human with the divine. Every step in the right direction is welcome and a mighty help to move you towards your goal. No effort is to be minimized; no step is too small as you take advantage of the avenues the Lord opens for you. Enter the doors He opens; get through them to the desired goal. Your tiny and imperfect effort—that is what the Lord will use to uplift and perfect you and your dreams. Such efforts, small as they may be, will be like the two fish and five loaves of barley made bread. With it, He will spring up the miracle of feeding the 5000. Your meager efforts are the grain, the mustard seed or stupendous growth in which the birds shall make their home; it is the seed planted which He will multiply in yield a hundredfold.

* * *

There is really no abstraction about this. Prayer is real and its effects are incontestable. As Alfred Lord Tennyson's persona says in the poem already referred to above, "More things are wrought by prayer than this world dreams of." To take from an example close to my heart and experience, my mother was a patient for almost as long as I knew her upon reaching an age to reason it out. Yes, she developed a kidney disease when I was still in elementary school. Sadness came on her and diffused itself to our entire household and broader family. Mommy was the rock of our family and anything happening to her was sure to be suicidal for the entire home—her children, parents, loved ones. But she had this one strength: she was very prayerful and resorted to prayer, her only hope. She prayed for herself, asked others to pray for her, and offered Masses that stormed heaven for her healing and return to good health. At my tender age, I had a simple prayer: "Lord, make mommy well."

It was as a last resort that her doctor, Professor Jacob Lifanji Ngu (M.D.), tried out a medication from Switzerland. The drug was new and certainly not yet much tested, but Mommy took it all the same. Was it Shakespeare who said, "Desperate diseases require desperate remedies"? She had no choice, given her precarious situation. Tests soon presented significant improvement in her condition. When he reviewed the tests results, Professor Ngu paced along the corridor in the hospital professing out loud "Ça, ç'est un miracle" ("This is a miracle"), adding: "Science cannot explain this."

My mother lived for about twenty-five more years and passed on at the age of 55, when we, her children and many of her dependents, had grown into mostly independent adults. I had finished my Ph.D. and about engaging application processes into medical school. Mommy spent those bonus twenty-five years coaching and caring for her loved ones as well as realizing her dreams of a more fulfilled life.

On my personal plain, when I moved to Nebraska to study at Creighton University, I had come to the US with little more than $1000 in my pocket upon my admission into that university. The then Graduate Students Director, Dr. Floyd Knoop, made it clear to me that the department had allotted all graduate student stipends; there was nothing left. It was pure anguish to contemplate my survival in the strange circumstances without financial assistance.

Already two weeks late for school when I got to Omaha, I had neither time nor the wherewithal to look for accommodation off campus. Dr. Knoop arranged for me to live on campus, in the freshman dormitory. I gratefully shared a room with a freshman. But the room and board was expensive, way beyond my financial resources as they stood. Yet, the advantages of living in the dormitory were not to be ignored. For the room and board cost included a meal plan, for which the University's Residence Life allowed a payment plan. Besides, not having a car, it was advantageous to live within strolling distance from the department; I saved myself the hassle of finding my way to class, if I rented an apartment off campus. It also meant that I did not have the stress of making rounds in search of an apartment to rent.

I focused on schoolwork and scouted for an on-campus job, praying the Lord God to provide one. I was not asking for much; just a little, enough to pay for my room and board; nothing more. Yet, for this I prayed without ceasing, filled out some applications and then waited. When one morning Dr. Knoop requested me to see him after lectures, I was not ready for it. I did not need anything more to worsen my condition, I thought, rather agitatedly and went to see him, butterflies in my stomach.

I ought to have rejoiced instead, for Dr. Knoop informed me that he had secured (in the department), some funds that would help me—$500 monthly. It was divine intervention. Tear-filled, I thanked him even as he apologized for not being able to secure something better. What he had secured, however, went a long way to ameliorate my financial situation. I could not wait to go before the Lord after classes to thank Him. Tears washed my entire face all through the prayer of gratitude I poured out to the Lord. I realized that I was special in God's eyes; that He cares for my personal and every need; that He has me in the palms of his hands and keeps close watch over me. We all are precious in the sight of the Lord, the psalmist says.

The warmth I felt, the assurance that pervaded my being is not a permanent thing. For sometimes we even have the feeling that God is not answering our prayers. Those are dry moments and can be very discouraging, bringing about the emotional downside, sadness and anxiety. The future becomes so uncertain that we look at it as bleak. Praying at such times is a matter of pure faith that all will be well. And this can last a while, days, weeks or even months. Those are moments of drought and maybe time for vicarious suffering for souls. That is perhaps the pattern we should expect, for like Christ, we are to suffer many tribulations as participants in the redemptive life he lived.

Saint Faustina, like other saints before and after her, kept thanking Jesus for the sufferings in her life (St, Faustina's Diary, Entry 343). But even in the drought, there filters a strong feeling of God's presence, love and care. Before long and suddenly, the layers of darkness peel off and an emotional thrill of relief takes over, inexplicably. Peace that the world cannot give sweeps over and we are back to the cozy folds of God's arms.

Just as there is need for persistence efforts to attain our goals, we ought to persevere in prayer, praying without ceasing, assured that God answers prayers; that He does so at the right time, His time. To be sure, His timetable often differs from our own. Why, even Christ did not have it easy, a thing indicated in His cry from the cross: "My God, my God, why hath thou forsaken me?"

Not only is His timetable different, His way, the right way, too, is different from ours. Yet, our pain and anguish are perfectly understood. For, Jesus, having gone through all he went through, truly understands our human plight. On our part, let us be assured that we can never be abandoned by Him in our sufferings, de-humaneness or indignity. If we nurse any doubts, it is to prayer we should go to obtain the grace to grow and remain strong in God.

Besides the over-sung need for living in the continuous presence of God, therefore, we need to involve God in all our decision-making processes. Seek the guidance of the Holy Spirit, an absolute necessity. Trying to be in the presence of God throughout even busy days is a way of involving God in everything we do. It has a reassuring and calming effect. In His presence, we are secure in the foundation of our being, which makes for authenticity and integrity. In that mood, the good, the happy, the sad or painful all fit in as His design and automatically become our choice as well.

* * *

One year, after the fall term, when schools were breaking up for Christmas holidays, I wanted to give a thank you gift to my children's bus drivers. They drove my children on the hour-long journey to and from school all year. From my dad who was visiting, I borrowed $100 for that purpose but instantly lost $50 which made me feel devastated. My dad, however, offered to me $50 more. I accepted and then made the gift to the bus drivers. When I picked up my children from the bus stop that afternoon, I lamented that I had not found the lost $50 and that I now owed dad $150. My ten-year-old son then said something which to me was remarkable, coming from him so young: "Mom, some days, when you wake up and something bad happens, it is your cross for the day. Christ carried a very heavy cross for us."

I turned to him and said, "So, are you saying that I should see losing this $50 as my cross for the day?"

Without hesitation, he replied, "Yes, mom."

I instantly stopped lamenting about the lost money, despite my empty wallet. Sometimes, our troubles are in our lament. Harping on them not only gives them substance but enlarges their presence. If the mishap is so overbearing that you cannot but morosely nurse and ruminate on it, do one smart thing besides: lift it up to God.

"Pray, hope and don't worry" is a caution attributed to St. (Padre) Pio and may well serve as a motto for us to take home. This introductory mention of Padre Pio and his mantra on hope initiates a necessity for a word on hope.

Hope

In the gospel of John, Jesus admonishes: "Do not let your hearts be troubled, trust in me," a clear recommendation for hope and being positive in the midst of the challenges we are pitched with.

Our hope comes from the cross of Jesus who surrendered himself to enter our lives in order to save us. The cross is a tall sign of the weight of our private difficulties. And Jesus who underwent the suffering of the cross knows what it feels like when the road seems weary and unbearable. He knows what it feels like when we feel abandoned, thanks to his anguished experience shouted out from the cross. Jesus understands what it means to feel exhausted, if you remember how tired he was as to sleep in the midst of the storm. Jesus understands human pain, which is very consoling, since he can thus journey with us through our humanness. He experienced rejection, injustice, abandonment. He knows what it means to live all these. So, we are in the company of a very experienced guide.

He also knows the value of compassion, having himself received it when Veronica wiped His face. The humility of accepting help from others is something he shared when Simon of Cyrene helped him to carry His cross. To desperate circumstances, Jesus is no stranger, having himself undergone the extremity of abandonment on the cross, as expressed in his voice: "My God, my God, why have you abandoned me?"

It is thus proper to see in the cross Jesus' solidarity with us and our humanity. There is no pain or anguish of ours that He would not understand. You therefore never have to feel alone in your sufferings; never let hopelessness overtake you. As Christ himself tells us: "Do not let your heart be troubled; do not be worried." On the principle which was elaborated on substitution, worries must be substituted with something. Praise is an apt substitution value for worry.

Praise

One way of yielding to God's will is to acknowledge his greatness and to praise Him. At the same time, praise is a mark of humility. We acknowledge our finiteness against His infinity. Praise thus fits into the enterprise of prayer rather snugly. As said earlier, the bottom line of prayer, all prayer, is about blending our will with God's. Praise is a way of not only saying, "You are awesome, O God, my Master," but also of saying: "I yield to all you will."

Praise, especially in song, moves the depth of emotions and commitment to the words and feel of the melody. Yet, praise can be expressed even without song by simple words— "Father, I praise you." "Lord, may your name be praised." In this pronouncement, we lift mind, heart and emotions along with our predicaments to Him.

Is not praise at the very heart and does it not constitute the essence of the Lord's Prayer? Notice the way it is wrapped and ensconced: "…Hallowed be thy name; Thy kingdom come; Thy will be done on earth as it is in heaven…" Praise here is strung up to voice out the fact that we, sons and daughters of our very own Father, are "yielded and still" for the Lord to act on us. *Thy will be done* is the same as the disposition: "Have Thine own way, Lord…Thou art the potter; I am the clay. Mould me and make me after thy will".

In praise we offer everything to the surpassing goodness that merits our praise, the greatness of God. To his majestic but loving and all-wise eminence we wisely surrender our all for His superior management.

Praise has the effect too of cheering up the one praising. Most obviously, this happens when we express ourselves in song. Bitterness yields to the cheerful voice in its admiration and song to the Maker. In praise, even enemies forget their differences and focus on the Lord who is worthy of all praise. Thus, bitterness is let go of and replaced by focus on the object of praise. That is why two violently opposed people can sing a beautifully harmonized duet. They let go of their differences in the process and focus on the praise or song effect. Praise prioritizes the object of praise over personal hurts and narrow concerns. By default, praise is a prayer for the grace of forgiveness of others. On the instant, anyone, even if s/he is the cause of a scorching challenge you are facing, is forgotten. In praise, anger and hurt are substituted for with joy, praise and honor to God. In praise, we let go the sin of the offender and concentrate on the object of our praise.

Of course, some hurts can outdo praise by shouting from the depth of our hearts. If you are having difficulty in letting go, go vocal and passionately commit the situation into prayers. If the ill-feelings are not so abrasive, gently turn them into prayer points. Your prayer can be as simple as,

> *Lord, you know how much this is eating me up, disturbing me. I feel awful that I find myself dwelling on this wrong done to me. But I find it hard to get rid of the painful thoughts. I am trying so hard to get rid of it, but it does not seem to be working. It keeps coming back. I offer these thoughts to you, Lord Jesus, humbly imploring you to rid me of them. Jesus, please, help me.*

I have found that when asked with sincerity of heart, these thoughts do go away; the Lord does answer. However, if they persist or even get worse, do not be discouraged. Only continue appealing to the Lord. It is not unusual that the more you try to get rid of bitterness and anger, the more they linger. Persist in trying by prayer and praise.

After the Storm

The journey to your goal does not end in merely getting rid of difficulties, whether by the help of others, by activated hope, prayer or praise. Admittedly, hanging in there, turning things around is quite an achievement, but it would be a pity if you left it there. Do not let the achievement get wasted. Strike out for the goal while using the process of the journey to help other people. Tug the hands and bear up the faltering steps of others who are stranded at the spot where you used to be or have been. Be a shoulder they can lean on, a source of strength and a mentor to them. Your journey of life is the more meaningful when it makes a difference in the life of others, if it saves others from despair.

The prayer of peace attributed to St. Francis of Assisi capture the mien expected of you anytime: "Lord make me an instrument of your peace….." It lists ways of being helpful to others and the application of these sentiments may include encouraging them, sharing your own story with them, positively using your position of influence, or simply speaking peace to them.

Words have power; you must remember that. They can hurt as they can heal; they can be balmy love or piercing, heart-rending swords; they can connect and unite as they can shatter and scatter.

When I arrived for a conference in 02/2017 in San Antonio, Texas, I was in my room before dinner and decided to call my family. My six-year-old daughter piped old wisdom to my listening ears: "Make sure you eat healthy food and remember my rule to think about what you want to say before you say it." Though funny, coming from a child, this is wisdom as profound and relevant as any wizened or aged philosopher can give. The gastronomic counsel is universal and the recommendation to watch one's words is perennial.

Words may be shifted or materialized into forms of assistance, in which case the advice is for us to use our experience helpfully for others. My encounter with one patient highlights this. She shared her son's exasperation in attempting to study medicine, but was troubled that he would not gain admission into medical school. He was at the verge of giving up, she said. He was doing a master's degree in Neuroscience as a dismally unsatisfactory alternative. I shared with her how my path to medical school had not been a straight one, but winding. Blocked by circumstances from even applying, I had proceeded to do a Doctorate degree, but had not closed my eyes on my dream of becoming an OB/Gyn physician. The detour took me away for some five years in which I studied for a different degree. It did not go down well with people who had no idea how I cherished my goal and they had plied reasons that aimed at killing that dream. The discouragement compounded the tasking time lapse. The terminal degree achieved, I yet passed one and a half more years in nondescript employment. Eventually, I attended medical school.

My story lighted hope in the patient's eyes and she described our encounter as "a prized patient visit". Two years on, when the same patient came for her annual gynecologic exam, tears streamed down her eyes. She said that her son held on to my story and was starting medical school in PA in the fall of that year. My story, mere words, had kept him going and changed his life, she said.

The story of your private survival strategy can ease the burden and fear of another person. Your unusual path of difficult times and how you overcame can be another person's strength over a desperate situation and the needed help towards their success. In any case, success breeds success; a success story diminishes desperation and generates hope for others.

The shared success story is an aspect of charity, of giving back to others what God enriches us with. We should not be selfish with our talents and experiences. And when we give, we must not expect reward but consider ourselves honored as instruments of God's purposes. Our instrumentality in God's plan has many channels of expression. In the rather small things of life, this can be very easy to take note of, if we become conscious of others' needs:

- Hear the cry of the poor; assist them.
- Hear the cry of the orphan and the widow; meet and respond to them.
- There are the brokenhearted; mend their hearts.
- There are the spirit-crushed; pick and patch them up.
- Make a difference in somebody's life; bring light to

others' darkness; keep their hope alive.

- Help them to override difficulties.
- Give them opportunities, perhaps by simply being the single voice or hand to occasion the life-transforming change and permanently so.

That God should use you to glorify His name, to fulfill His purpose in the lives of others; that you should be light for others, making them feel your touch as of an angel: that should be your prayer. For this I pray, at the same time trying to remember to praise and be thankful to God for the many things he does and is doing in my life and yours. And that is what prayer can really mean—invoking, being with, silence, ridding the self of negative emotions by putting positive actions in their place, praising, hoping, being meaningful by giving meaning and assistance to others.

Prayer becomes life, the word whispered by God, His will, your active participation in bringing about His kingdom on earth. It means listening to the rhythm of creation and joining in, not just to make a noise, but to create harmony. With harmony, every aspect fits into place and growth is enabled. Prayer becomes self-gift, which is not such an easy thing. Sometimes it takes a lot to arrive at such wisdom and I am a sure witness as narrated in the next chapter.

CHAPTER SIX

THE FINALE OF GOALS - SELF-GIFT

My going to England after high school at the age of eighteen was the first time I was leaving my parents for over three months at a time. While I was excited to see the horizons of the Western hemisphere and to further my education, I was also nervous. Going to a foreign land, thousands of kilometers away, wasn't a stroll in the backyard of our house. The thought of leaving my parents was daunting. So, I was no longer going to see them often, not even yearly! It was hard, the sister of, or the match of something akin to death.

Similarities in some African puzzles and expressions are captured in the image of brother/sister. The sister of death, for example is sleep. My going away for so long was the sister of death in a very real sense. With it came grief, for all loss engenders such nostalgic sadness. And I didn't have the monopoly of grief for I could see the pain in my mother's eyes as well. When she gave me one last hug at the Douala airport, just before I walked down the long tunnel to join my international flight, I felt her pain and knew tears weren't far from her eyes. It was a walk into independence for me but it felt too early and coming on rather precipitous. It was emotionally and physically challenging, a kind of death or my feeling about it, my perception. The perception, which did not come abruptly or as a surprise, yet had disruptive consequences. It was jarring and painful, stirring the profoundest feeling of nostalgia and loss.

The grief shaded into other feelings. Initially, I would get very homesick and lonely. However, I had a good network of support and stayed focused on what I came to the University of London for: I had a goal to work towards. I spent my holidays with one of dad's cousins, a helpful connectivity with my family. It was a great help to have family around. Buoyed by these scaffolds, I gradually progressed from obtaining a BSc to an MSc. But that was as good as it could be for shock waves soon rocked my boat.

To get the texture of how I was going to feel, it is important to peep into my childhood, an enriching and rewarding one in which I very closely bonded with my maternal grandparents. They were dotingly fond of me as of their other grandchildren. We spent our Christmases and summer holidays with them, each time engaged in a multitude of activities. We attended our all-village traditional dance (which advantageously held every Christmas holiday period) and Christmas time was really family thrill.

Summer was generally time for farm work and in our own small way we took part in all that went on in the farms as well—plowing, planting, weeding and harvesting. We helped harvest coffee beans, drying and selecting them as well as run errands for our grandparents. With them, we socialized with other family members.

Ours was a close knit family. It was hard to tell apart the members; you couldn't tell from our interactions that everyone was not from the same mother and father. So, even after two years in England, when I went home for summer holidays and spent time with my grandparents, it was, as always, absolute delight.

The devastation can be imagined when on Christmas Day 1989 I received a phone call that my maternal grandfather had died that early morning. The shock was the more shattering in that we had, until then, been blessed that none of my close relatives in living memory had passed away. To lose my dear maternal grandfather, who was a vital part of my young life, was really tragic. From the transitory absence I had experienced in travelling far away, something more sinister now came: death itself, not its *sister*.

I could not believe that I would never see him in the flesh again, that I would not hear his voice. Emptiness dug a hole in my heart and sadness entered it. I was not going to be there to see him at home one last time before his burial. I would have loved that closure, which is like a ritual of forgetfulness. Psychologists recommend such closing ceremonies, so to say. It is the wisdom of anniversary celebrations and sackcloth removal events; they put a seal on grief for new life to kick start. The next year was hard for me, although that was child's play when measured against what was to come later.

Ten years on, in 1999, there was excitement in the air as the world looked forward to the closure of one century and entry through the door of a new century and millennium. History was marking itself out for the long coverage of years and happenings—two World Wars and attempts to stem the Third. There was reason to expect that that Third World War would be halted, especially as in 1991 Gorbachev had introduced the *glasnost* and *perestroika* into the Soviet system. In addition, there had been a series of revolutions across the Soviet Bloc states in 1989. Without the Cold War, a Third World War lacked an immediate reason to start.

While the world bathed in joyful expectancy, I received a dreadful phone call: my aunt (my mother's immediate follower) had died suddenly. I was rocked by the jolting news emotionally and psychologically. I cried and cried. It was the second death of a close family member, another one who had been an intimate part of my life and upbringing. Her perennially beautiful smile and gentle voice kept playing over and over in my head. A dull grieving held me tight, but more, I worried about how this would affect mother, her siblings and us, the children. I worried about the impact of my aunt's death on my grandmother, how difficult it is to bury one's child! Fear gripped me.

That fear hovered and virtually settled as part of my psyche. I was struggling to deal with the embarrassment of losing my aunt, vaguely hoping against hope that life would somehow rekindle sunshine for my family. My coping strategies were still in their crude infancy three months on.

Yes, exactly three months on, on September 15th 1999, my phone rang at 02.32 am. It was an eerie hour for a call. I picked it up. At the other end of the line was our family friend, Mr. Bertrand Eyoum, whom we called Ton-ton Berto – French for "Uncle Berto". He was of Douala origin and not into the niceties of psychological cushioning, typical of my Grassfield people of the North West Region in Cameroon. He was in a haste to trigger the missile. Well, I had no idea and perhaps dragged the delivery a little too slow for his urgent message. Yet the conversation was succinct; unforgettably, exactly as follows:

Me: "Hello".

Ton-ton Berto: "Adeline, c'est Ton-ton Berto." ("Adeline, this is uncle Berto").

Me: "Ah, Ton-ton, bonjour." ("Ah, uncle, good morning").

Ton-ton Berto: "Quel heure est-il?" ("What time is it?").

Me: "Il est deux heures, trente-deux" ("It is two thirty-two").

Ton-ton Berto: "Flo est morte. Mes condoléances" ("Flo is dead. My condolences").

The call ended and the ensuing silence shouted crassly bizarre and discordant tunes.

Flo was my mom, Florence.

To this day, I cannot find words to describe the feeling that surged through me. Was this real? Denial. Did I just have a bad dream? Some form of allowing for a distorted possibility. Did I just hear Ton-ton Berto say what he said? Utter disbelief. Ton-ton just told me that my mother had died. I swirled, confused.

Only about a week before, I had talked with her and she was readying to travel to the United States and me in two weeks. This could not be true. Just three months since my aunt died—how cruel!

No matter how much I disbelieved or detested it, my mother was indeed dead. It was an icy fact and the essentials had to be done. It did not matter that my emotions sizzled and jerked in spasms of radical shock; that my heart was jumpy every so often; that my thought quivered and attempted to recoil at the least hint of the fact being a fact. My countenance flared in disbelief but my eyes kept steady effusions of hot tears.

There was no time to be lost. Arrangements were soon completed for the sad trip back home for the burial ceremonies. The flight was hard, dull and stretched forever, unlike any other I had before made to or from home. When we landed in Douala airport, I burst into tears as the emotions of my parting goodbyes and recalled hot motherly welcome embraces at the vicinity came drenching me.

My mother would usually be there beaming her heart-warming smile, all joy and waiting to enfold me in her capacious heart with many hugs. We would exchange stories and small talk. Not so today. Cruel reality struck home: mommy was no longer there; she was in the cold mortuary. We eventually arrived in Bertoua (where my parents were living at the time). If my mother's absence at the airport was negative proof, her corpse was incontestable reality. It sank home, shot straight to my trembling heart and stirred it with vicious twerks. I agonized unconsolably. A huge part of me was gone. Only a flimsy and lonely remnant tripped back to the US after the funeral.

Life was hardly life any longer, my mother, my anchor, my best friend snatched away. She had helped me to navigate through life; she had been the rock I leaned on, my stronghold in the rough bumps of the road of life. Could life be so cruel? Depression descended on me and it became hard to do anything, nay, everything—to get up in the morning, study, work, smile, find joy or meaning to life. Even eating became irrelevant and sleep abandoned me. One year after, I was still in depression: I would come home, slump onto the couch and stare at the walls all night. It was a lucky day if I got four hours of continuous sleep.

I lost all interest in life; lost all zeal. My hope was gone, my right hand trimmed off, as it were. Tears were uncontrollably unstoppable and for days unend. My mind and memories halted on mom and my heart ached, missing her in extremis.

My one desire was to be with her. Without her, life came to a halt. My friends came to attempt my rescue, spending enormous time with me. They would take me to their houses for a few days, but I was stuck in grief, impervious to any form of consolation. My family too buckled up to help, said all they considered worth saying. But water on a duck's back sticks easier than their words would move me. Grief ate me, embittered and angered me that my beloved aunt, and then my mother, should be snatched away in such a quick succession. What promise was there that anything else that mattered to me could last? I saw life as callous, cruel and unfair.

In hindsight, it is a wonder that I bore it through; that I eventually could deal with the grief and move on. I attribute this quietly miraculous evolution to the prayers of my friends and family who never gave up. It is a point of eternal gratitude for me for their relentless storming of heaven.

The turning point came with a brief thought in a defining moment—my grandmother. She too had been devastated and still grieved the loss of her first two children only months apart. Hard luck, it must have been really tough for her. What sorrow for any mother! Now the question welled up from deep within me: What if grandmother also gave up on life? Her other living children and us, her grandchildren, were all she had. She had lost her husband many years before.

Now I worried about my grandmother; saw her grieving face. That was the twist that made me think a little differently that day: maybe I had to be strong for her. Perhaps, we (her grandchildren) were her glimmer of hope and strength to carry on. Now it struck home: I had to revive and go on for her sake. I might encourage her to go on. The way to do that was for me to also try to go on in positive strides. It was impossible for me to be there for *mamun* (as we called her) when I had lost all control myself?

The connection between my grandmother and the surviving siblings of my mother came easy. I started feeling for them, how hard it really was for them too. Besides their own grief, they were worried about me and my cousins. Maybe I could give them a little relief by making an effort to take life more proactively. They would have one less thing to worry about.

That is how, slowly, over time, I started coping with the pain of my loss. It was only a little step each time in that direction, each very helpful. So I began to realize that pain does not go away: you learn to live and cope with it, bending away and blunting its sharp edges from crippling or killing you.

* * *

And so, when your goal is set, when challenges to achieving it are converted to opportunities through decisiveness, action and the right attitude; when we have tapped from the encouragement of others and cultivated faith in the self, killing personal or extraneous inhibitions; when we have dug in our feet to patiently persist in the path of the goal; when we have let go of grudges and logged in on prayer, whether silent, meditative, oral or contemplative; when praise has acknowledged our place in life and dedicated all glory to our God, one thing will uplift our actions and ground our purpose resolutely—concern for others, charity to others, selfless service.

This is a thing we need not fumble into the way I did during my deep grief. It is self-gift; it is doing the little we can for others that constitutes the saving grace. Remember that the whole drama of life is to see how we expend ourselves in an authentic, effective and fruitful manner. That expending of the self is best captured in the service we render, the concern we have for others. It is the forgetting of our indignities, grief, petty self-love and focusing on others. Granted, it is hard to jump straight into self-giving without haltering steps in self-indulgence, but it is important to target selflessness as our life project. In fact, the enterprise of goal setting derives its value and legitimacy from this one focal design: *self-gift*.

ACKNOWLEDGEMENT

This book was edited by *PATAMAE* Research and Editing Consultancy. I would like to thank Paddy, my amazing editor, for his professional advice along with crisp and meticulous editing.

Words cannot express my gratitude to my husband, Godfrey (ND) for his unwavering loving support and encouragement. I thank him for his help in every way that allows me to engage in new projects. My dear, you are incredible.

Special thanks to my children Divine, Kamabesen, and Florence, who remind me that one can get up everyday and rewrite his or her legacy, and that everyday is a new day. I thank them for putting up with me when I am distracted and for their unconditional love and support. You continually make my journey worthwhile.

ABOUT THE AUTHOR

Fellow of the American College of Obstetricians and Gynecologists (practicing Obstetrician & Gynecologist), Dr. Adeline Nukuna obtained an MD and a PhD from the Creighton University School of Medicine, Omaha, Nebraska after a BSc and MSc from the University of London.

Adeline is a married mother of three who treasures family time, writing, travel and opportunities for positive impact on lives — thus impassioned with service to others, as healthcare provider and the general challenges of life. Keen on impressing upon individuals to take responsibility for their health and life as a package, she has been guest speaker at educational institutions and community events, contributing articles for newspapers and women's magazines on this. In from *Low to Glow: Shaping the Rhythm of Creation by Self-Gift* she explores profound life adjustment and coping practices.

Made in the USA
Monee, IL
08 July 2021

72561214R00080